GOVERNMENT IN
H-CENTURY IRELAND

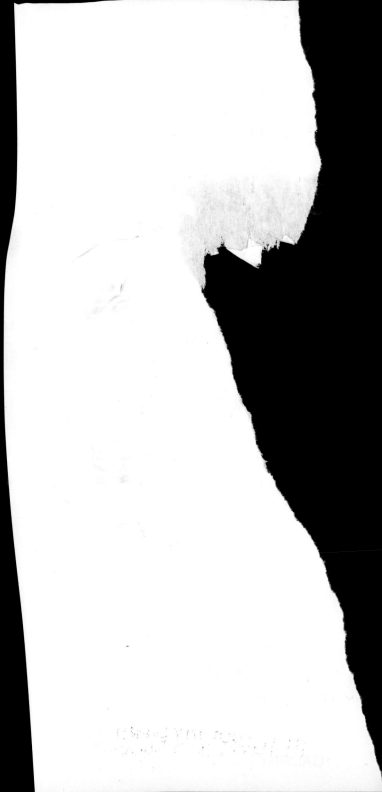

Local Government in Nineteenth-century Ireland

Virginia Crossman

The Institute of Irish Studies
The Queen's University of Belfast
for the Ulster Society of Irish Historical Studies

Published 1994
The Institute of Irish Studies
The Queen's University of Belfast
for the Ulster Society of Irish Historical Studies

British Library Cataloguing-in-Publication Date. A catalogue card for this book is available for the British Library.

ISBN 085389 5090

Printed by W & G Baird Ltd, Antrim.
Cover design by Rodney Miller Associates.

Contents

Acknowledgments

I wish to acknowledge the generous financial assistance given by the Department of Education, Northern Ireland, towards the costs of producing this book. Support was also received from the Cultural Traditions Programme of the Community Relations Council, which aims to encourage acceptance and understanding of cultural diversity. Preliminary research was undertaken at the Institute of Irish Studies, at the Queen's University of Belfast. My thanks are due to the staff of the following libraries and record offices: the Public Record Office of Northern Ireland; the National Library of Ireland; the National Archives, Dublin; the Public Record Office, London; the British Library; Staffordshire Record Office; Liverpool Record Office and the Bodleian Library, Oxford. For permission to cite material from the Morpeth papers I am grateful to the Hon. Simon Howard. Publication would have been impossible without the support of the Ulster Society for Irish Historical Studies, and the commitment and encouragement of Dr Margaret Crawford. Maria Luddy gave me the benefit of her unrivalled knowledge of sources for Irish women's history. For this (and much more) I am grateful.

Introduction

Throughout the nineteenth century the manner in which local government in Ireland was conducted was the focus of political discussion and debate. In the early years of the century, when positions of local responsibility were held almost exclusively by members of the Protestant landed elite, local government was a major source of grievance within the catholic community. Local government reform was one of the demands of catholic leaders such as Daniel O'Connell, who sought admittance to the grand jury room and the corporation chamber. As the century progressed and the opportunities for Catholics to become involved in local administration became more numerous, most notably with the introduction of elections for town commissioners, members of municipal corporations and poor law guardians, local government became an important proving ground for nationalist politicians. Local elections provided an opportunity to debate national as well as local issues, and meetings of local bodies increasingly became the scenes of party politcal conflict and manoeuvring. By the closing decades of the century local self-government was being pursued both as an alternative and as a stepping stone to national self-government.

As far as government ministers were concerned dissatisfaction with the forms and the functionaries of local government could not be dismissed as a matter only of local concern. It was felt to taint government in general, with the result that people had little confidence in government or the law to protect their interests. The belief that by improving local administration and thereby winning the confidence of the people, lawlessness and turbulence would disappear from Ireland, and with them the clamour for separation from England, provided the impetus behind much local government reform in the nineteenth century. The problem was that until the very end of the nineteenth century, reform in the shape of local democracy, except in the most limited sense, was unacceptable to those governing Ireland. The alternative was to take more power into the hands of central government. Government officials were assumed to be both more efficient and more impartial administrators than protestant landowners and the growth of offices such as those of assistant barrister (to chair quarter sessions), stipendiary magistrate and inspector of prisons did reflect an increasing degree of intervention by central government in local affairs. But ministers never abandoned their commitment to the principle of local autonomy. Stipendiary magistrates, for example, were originally appointed only as a temporary expedient which, it was hoped, could be abandoned when the state of Ireland more nearly resembled the peace and good order which were believed to reign in England.

Local government in the modern sense did not exist at the beginning of the nineteenth century. For much of the century the role of government, whether central or local, was conceived as being extremely limited. Its main responsibility was to safeguard the lives and property of the people, allowing them to pursue their own interests within a stable and well-ordered community. The earliest representatives of central authority in the localities, the county sheriff and the local magistrates, were adjuncts of the legal system imported to Ireland from England. The office of high sheriff was introduced to Ireland in the reign of King John, although it was not until that of James I that it extended throughout the country.[1] Under the Plantagenets the whole machinery of local government and county administration was, in practice, centred on the sheriff. He selected the grand jury of the county, acted as president (but not judge) of the county court and served as the revenue collector for the royal exchequer. The grand jury was the body responsible for presenting criminals within the county for trial. Made up of the leading gentlemen of the county, the jury heard evidence and decided whether a prima facie case existed. Justices of the peace, who like the sheriff were appointed by the crown, took informations relating to crimes committed in their neighbourhoods and tried cases brought before them at petty or quarter sessions.

From the seventeenth century onwards the grand jury acquired a wide range of administrative functions. These grew out of the power of grand juries to present defaults in roads and bridges constituting the king's highway, and to levy a fine on the inhabitants of the district to enable the damage to be repaired. In 1634 parliament passed an act enabling judges at assize, with the consent of the grand jury and justices of the peace assembled at quarter sessions, to tax the inhabitants of their respective districts for the purpose of constructing or repairing causeways or bridges. This was the beginning of the presentment system and of local taxation to fund public services. The following year grand juries were empowered to pass presentments for the building and maintenance of one or more houses of correction in each county. But it was not until the eighteenth century that the grand jury was confirmed as the central organ of local government. Formerly justices of the peace sitting at quarter sessions acted in conjunction with the grand jury in matters of local administration, but in 1727 parliament decreed that presentments could be made at the assizes only and not at quarter sessions. Further acts extended the ambit of the grand jury to include the construction and maintenance of hospitals and lunatic asylums, the support of dispensaries, the relief of the poor and the payment of police.[2] By the time of the union with England in 1800, grand juries had become an important feature of county life and were responsible for considerable amounts of money. (Grand jury presentments totalled around £400,000 in 1803.)[3] A major portion of this was accounted for by the salaries of the various officials on the grand jury payroll, from the secretary and treasurer of the grand jury itself to the sub-constables of the county. The grand jury was not, however, the only taxing authority in an Irish county. Vestry tax was levied in some ecclesiastical parishes. Local records from various Ulster parishes indicate that vestry cess was being raised well into the nineteenth century for a variety of purposes. The vestry book of the parish of Arboe in County Tyrone for the period 1773 to 1833, for example, reveals that vestry cess was levied for the repair and upkeep of the church and church hall, for the care of deserted and exposed children and for providing coffins for the poor.[4]

The main components of local government in Ireland derived from English models. The civil distribution of Ireland was, however, very different from that of England. In England the most important administrative units were the parish and the county. Ireland was divided into townlands, parishes, baronies, counties and provinces. Townlands were the smallest (and earliest) territorial division, which, grouped together, made up baronies, similar to English hundreds. Baronies formed sub-divisions of counties and counties of provinces. Parishes were relatively little used in Ireland for civil purposes, although they did form the basis of petty sessions districts and for levying fines imposed for malicious damage of property. (There were, of course, two separate parochial structures in Ireland from the Reformation onwards. The old medieval parishes became civil parishes, and parishes of the Established Church, while the Catholic Church developed a new parochial organisation.) As the machinery of local government grew more complex over the course of the nineteenth century new units and divisions were superimposed onto the existing structure, the most important of these being the poor law union. As far as urban government was concerned, the exemplar was once again an English one. The Anglo-Normans established a network of municipalities based on the English chartered borough, which embraced both existing towns and those newly created during the conquest of Ireland. Towns were granted royal charters which conferred upon them the privilege of self-government. They could elect officers and councils, appoint magistrates, set up courts, control industry and make laws and ordinances for the good government of the town. Another important feature of the boroughs was their right to send representatives to the parliaments or public councils held in Ireland. Anxious to increase their influence within the Irish house of commons the Stuart kings, James I and Charles II, created a considerable number of new corporations in the sevententh century, whose charters vested power in small groups (the free burgesses) instead of in the citizens as a body as the earlier charters of incorporation had done. By the time of the Union in 1800, most corporations bore a closer resemblance to exclusive clubs, with membership often restricted to individuals drawn from a single family, than to governing bodies. Many existed in name only and for the sole purpose of returning MPs to the Irish parliament. With the abolition of the latter in 1800 and the reduction in the number of parliamentary constituencies, thirty-six corporate boroughs disappeared, leaving sixty-three corporations presiding over places as diverse as Dublin, Kinsale and Carrickfergus.[5]

The Union thus had a direct impact on municipal government. Thirty corporations became extinct subsequent to the act of union, leaving the inhabitants of these places without even the most basic of local services, such as the means to regulate markets and tolls. County administration was not directly affected, but as the nineteenth century progressed its conduct was to be subject to increasing scrutiny and criticism by MPs at Westminister. While even the most progressive English politicians believed that the Irish required considerable coaching in the art of government, and many openly doubted their capacity to administer their own affairs with any degree of efficiency given the divisions within Irish society, it became increasingly difficult for MPs to tolerate a situation in which the vast majority of the Irish population were excluded from any say in the conduct of local affairs. Parliamentary inquiries and literary accounts present a picture of a country where power was vested in a landed elite whose members too often regarded local government as source of personal status and influence, not as a civic responsibility. Reform in some shape or form could hardly be avoided and the first half of the nineteenth century saw the introduction of democratically elected municipal corporations and the elimination of the worst examples of inefficiency and graft perpetrated by grand juries. During the second half of the century a massive expansion in the remit of local government, as local authorities were forced to take on new responsibilities regarding public health and welfare, acted as a catalyst for reform. Irish measures were considered separately from those affecting England, but English models continued to shape Irish legislation. Both the municipal reform act of 1840 and the local government act of 1898 owed much to English precedent. Indeed it was the declared aim of many English reformers to bring Irish practice more closely into line with English. How closely depended on the extent to which they were prepared to see power pass into the hands of the catholic community. Concern on this head lay behind the opposition to reform proposals throughout the century and explains the reluctance with which English ministers embraced the principle of democratisation at local level. Where ratepayers were granted a say in local affairs this was generally accompanied by an element of central supervision. Thus the poor law boards created in 1838 to administer poor relief, and comprising partly of ex officio guardians drawn from the local magistracy and partly of guardians directly elected by ratepayers, operated under the watchful eye of the poor law commissioners, a government-appointed body.[6] Reform of local government took place on a piecemeal basis. Established institutions were overhauled and new bodies tacked onto the existing structure to cope with the expanding limits of government responsibility. The resulting patchwork was a frankenstein's monster of overlapping authorities and jurisdictions. To explain how this came about and to identify the different organs of the local body politic and how they worked is the object of this pamphlet.

The work is divided into three sections. The first examines local government in rural areas and includes discussion of the role of county dignitaries such as the high sheriff and the lord lieutenant of the county, before moving on to consider the administrative work of grand juries and poor law boards. The second section covers local government in urban districts and describes the development of urban government under town commissioners and municipal corporations. The final section describes the changes brought about by the local government reform act of 1898. Within each section an attempt is made to trace administrative developments and legislative reforms over the course of the century and to locate them within the changing political scenery of nineteenth-century Ireland. The appendices include the holders of county lieutenancies in the period from 1831 to 1850, a list local government offices in existence at the end of the nineteenth century, and examples, drawn from across the country and across the century, of a grand jury, a board of poor law guardians, a town commission and a municipal corporation. Limitations imposed both by space and by the state of current research have meant that it has not been possible to provide an analysis of the membership of local government bodies or of their performance. The aim has been to describe the framework within which local government operated. The resulting pamphlet is in the nature of a sketch map; the real survey work, upon which more detailed mapping exercises must depend, remains to be done.

Published works on Irish local government are scarce and tend to be limited to particular aspects of local administration, such as the history of a municipal corporation or the management of a poor law union.[7] Much of the following discussion, therefore, relies on primary source material. Sources utilised include the records of grand juries, town commissioners and poor law boards together with private correspondence and newspaper reports relating to their activities. Parliamentary papers have been extensively used. These are an invaluable source for the historian of local government. The royal commission on municipal corporations, for example, remains one of the best sources of information relating to the early history of many Irish corporations.[8] Early nineteenth-century select committees appointed to report on the grand jury system, and those apppointed later in the century to investigate urban government, provide a unique window on the conduct of local administration. Where secondary sources are available they have been consulted, as will be apparent from the sections on poor law administration and municipal corporations which have drawn on the work of a number of historians working in these areas. Many of the primary sources quoted refer to counties in northern Ireland. This reflects both the particularly rich vein of local records to be found in the Public Record Office of Northern Ireland, and the location of the author, who was based in Belfast for much of the period during which the research for this pamphlet was undertaken. Although it would be unwise to present political activity in northern Irish counties as typical of the country as a whole, as far as the administrative activities of local bodies are concerned, examples drawn from these counties are generally applicable.

Notes

1   C.L. Falkiner, *The Counties of Ireland: an historical sketch of their origin, constitution and gradual delimitation* (Dublin, 1903).
2   See below, pp 35–36, and p. 69.
3   *First report from the select committee on grand jury presentments, Ireland*, H.C. 1822 (353), vii, 1.
4   Vestry book of Arboe, County Tyrone, 1773–1833 (P.R.O.N.I., Records of Arboe parish, D1278/1).
5   J.J. Webb, *Municipal Government in Ireland – Medieval and Modern* (Dublin, 1918).
6   See below, pp 64–65.
7   *First report of the commissioners appointed to inquire into the municipal corporations in Ireland*, H.C. 1835 (23), xxvii, *Supplement to the first report*, H.C. 1835 (24, 27, 28), xxvii; 1836 (29), xxiv.
8   Two recent examples are Sean O'Donnell, 'The first election to the reformed Clonmel Corporation 150 years ago' and Thomas Deegan, 'Roscrea Poor Law Union: its administration 150 years ago' in *Tipperary Historical Journal 1992*, 75–80, 96–104.

SECTION I:

Local Government in Rural Areas
A. County Officers

The High Sheriff

The high sheriff was the principal representative of central government in the county in relation to the execution of the law, being responsible for the execution of legal process in both civil and criminal actions issuing from the courts. His duties included selecting the grand jury and supervising the conduct of parliamentary elections. The extensive fiscal duties formerly performed by the sheriff as the king's bailiff had by the nineteenth century largely been transferred to the collectors of excise, but he remained responsible for levying debts due to the crown. The sheriff enjoyed magisterial powers which, as the report of a crown commission noted in 1826, were 'of the highest and most dignified description' but which in practice were rarely called into action, the preservation of the peace in disturbed districts having been effectively transferred to the police.[1] The sheriff nevertheless remained an important figure in the legal administration of the county and as such could be called upon to take an active role in maintaining order and upholding the authority of the law.

Sheriffs were appointed by the lord lieutenant. At the beginning of the century the usual practice was for the serving sheriff to name three suitable successors. These names were passed to the judge of assize on the summer circuit, who passed them to the lord chancellor who presented them to the lord lieutenant, the latter normally, though not invariably, appointing the first name on the list. The most important influence over nominations, in the early decades of the century at least, lay with county MPs who used the office as a source of political patronage. The politicization of the shrievalty attracted much criticism. Writing to a potential candidate for the office in Clare in 1814, the MP for the county, Vesey Fitzgerald, referred to the 'absolute prostitution' of the shrievalty in Clare which had left 'the gentry of the county excluded from their natural right [of serving on the grand jury], and the impanelling of juries made part of a political system'.[2] Fitzgerald approached various individuals requesting them to serve as sheriff for Clare. Unfortunately all his chosen candidates declined the offer.[3] During the chief secretaryship of Robert Peel, directions were given that the assize judge rather than the serving sheriff should compile a list of suitably qualified candidates for the ensuing year. The names returned were subsequently discussed by all twelve judges together with the lord chancellor and changes made if such were thought to be necessary. The final lists were laid before the lord lieutenant as before. Peel referred to the new practice during a debate on grand jury reform in 1817, insisting that party considerations no longer had any weight in the matter of sheriffs' appointments. He admitted that in some instances the out-going sheriff still made out the list but denied that this was always the case. Peel revealed that he had written to the lord chancellor as to the expediency of the instructing judges to return persons recommended by the grand jury, as in England, but nothing seems to have come of this.[4] Peel's reforms seem to have had some effect. A correspondent of Lord Sligo pronouncing on 'the causes of revolution all around us', in 1826, cited the first cause as 'Mr Peel's most timely and wise change in the sheriffs . . . which upset the whole machinery of old times'.[5]

As Fitzgerald's experience demonstrates, it was not always easy to find men to serve as high sheriff. Although there were no specific residence or property qualifications, candidates were normally landed gentlemen and were expected to be resident in the county for which they were nominated. They also needed to possess ample disposable income. Upon his appointment the sheriff was required to enter into a recognizance to the crown in a sum of £1,000 before the barons of exchequer. During the course of his year in office he would have to provide salaries for a returning officer (who acted as a kind of sheriff's clerk) and for sheriff's bailiffs and, in most cases, for an under- or sub-sheriff to perform the day to day duties of the office. The financial burden was considerable and could be ruinous. If a debtor escaped from a sheriff's bailiff, the sheriff was liable to be sued by the creditor for the sum involved. Sheriffs were answerable for the acts of their deputies and although securities were usually required from the latter, when tested these often proved worthless. Under these circumstances it was hardly surprising that many potential candidates were anxious to avoid the office. In 1808, Henry Brabazon had declined the offer of the Louth shrievalty, explaining to John Foster, MP for the county, that he could not afford to lose the '£300 or £400 which filling the office would at least cost'.[6] Two years later Foster found it necessary to write to Wallop Brabazon to elicit his help in finding someone to serve as sheriff, two possible candidates, including Henry Brabazon, having already refused while a third was not resident in Ireland.[7] Wallop Brabazon had nothing but sympathy for those who had refused: 'the insults gentlemen who serve the office receive from the secondaries in the court of exchequer are enough to deter any man of respectability from undertaking the office'. He recalled that he had been arrested at his wife's grave in the midst of his servants and tenants for a defalcation of £30. Sorting the matter out had cost him £400.[8] Eventually Henry Brabazon was prevailed upon to accept. He was summoned to Dublin where he found, as he later told Foster, that since 'nothing I could offer as an excuse would be admitted, I had no other alternative but to serve or leave the County in the lurch which I should be very sorry to do'.[9] Clearly it would be wrong to exaggerate the reluctance on the part of the Irish gentry to serve as sheriffs, since there was much to be gained in terms of personal and political influence, but the financial cost continued to provoke protests. In 1831 George Stoddart, the high sheriff of County Clare, petitioned the government for aid in meeting expenses incurred during his year in office. He had had no notice of his appointment since his name had not appeared on the list given by the outgoing sheriff to the judges and consequently he was 'quite unprepared for the expenses of even an ordinary year, how much less so for such a year as this when I had the expense of attending the judges with horses, carriage and servants for two assizes, an adjourned assizes and two [special] commissions, besides two contested elections'. His property, he added, was very small and the agitated state of the country had made it difficult, and in many cases impossible, to get at. Stoddart's request was refused.[10]

The powers invested in sheriffs and their deputies were notoriously abused. In the course of their inquiry in 1825, the commissioners appointed to inquire into the duties and emoluments of the sheriff's office identified abuses and irregularities which they believed had a direct tendency to obstruct the administration of justice and 'often to pervert it into a grievous source of oppression'. They stressed, however, that while their report probably underestimated the extent of the problem in some counties, in others 'principally in the Province of Ulster, we have reason to think that the office has been administered, comparatively, with correctness'.[11] The major problem lay with sub-sheriffs and bailiffs who exploited their position for financial gain. The commisioners found that although the profits of the sub-sheriff's office deriving from such fees as were considered legal or customary, were very inadequate some sub-sheriffs managed to make considerable amounts of money, most commonly by obtaining money from debtors in return for aiding them to escape their creditors. Sub-sheriffs were not supposed to serve for longer than one year at a time, with three years elapsing before a further term could be served, but this limitation was widely ignored. Sheriffs generally preferred to appoint a deputy who had proven experience of the work involved. The commissioners produced evidence of systematic dealing between sub-sheriffs and distressed property-owners to delay and obstruct creditors:

in many counties in Ireland there are individuals possessing residences
and establishments, and thus holding forth a show, which induces credit,
against whose persons or goods writs, though repeatedly lodged in the
sheriff's office, are seldom executed; or, if at all, after lengthened post-
ponement and great expense to their creditors.[12]

It was not only sub-sheriffs who were tempted to profit from their
position. Connel O'Donel, who served as high sheriff of Mayo in both
1813 and 1814, and who employed no deputy, was stated to have
appropriated money levied under executions to his own use. According to a resident of the county, O'Donel came to an understanding
with one local landowner, Colonel Brown, that writs were not to be
executed against him, 'but that afterwards they quarrelled and
Colonel Brown's goods were then sold, at which sale Mr O'Donel
became himself the purchaser of a quantity of wine; notwithstanding
which, the plaintiff, as I have been informed, has never been paid'.[13]

The commissioners made a number of recommendations for
reforming the sheriff's office, the most important of which was to
divest it of most of its ministerial duties, principally the execution of
legal process, and to transfer these to a crown officer who would operate under the supervision of the courts and would be removeable by
their order in the event of malfeasance or incompetence.[14] Ministers
from both the major parties were to prove reluctant to undertake so
drastic a reform. In 1828 Thomas Spring Rice, who had appeared
before the commissioners to give evidence about maladministration
by the sheriffs of Limerick city, and who was now a junior minister in
the home office, wrote to William Lamb, the chief secretary, to urge
him to act on the commissioners' report. The exigency of the case was
admitted, he pointed out, so why hesitate in giving a remedy?[15] Lamb
was caution personified. It was not sufficient, he maintained, merely
to identify an abuse and, while the suggestions of the report could easily be carried into effect, they had to consider carefully before changing the whole mode of executing the law and the constitution of the
sheriff's office. It was a mistake to attempt to do too much at once, for
in doing so they risked discrediting important reformations.[16] Lamb's
attitude seems to have been shared by his successors for despite
repeated declarations of intent it was not until 1835 that a measure
actually reached the statute book. This was a modest bill, falling far
short of the recommendations of the 1826 report. Sheriffs were no
longer required to obtain letters patent upon their appointment,
appointments of sub-sheriffs were to be in writing with copies sent to
the court of exchequer, and the rule prohibiting sub-sheriffs from
serving for more than one year was discontinued. Out-going sheriffs
were to give a list of all prisoners and writs under their charge to their
successors and stricter accounting regulations were introduced.[17]

The issue of public confidence was one which continued to concern government. In their report the commissioners had rejected allegations of improper selection of juries, both grand and petty, by sheriffs, observing that the care now taken by judges in the nomination of sheriffs ensured that respectable persons were appointed and proper jury panels returned. There was, they declared, no intentional exclusion of any particular class of gentry on the ground of either party or religious distinction.[18] But with sheriffs still being drawn almost exclusively from the protestant community, popular opinion remained obstinately sceptical on this point. The nomination of sheriffs, O'Connell exhorted the lord lieutenant, Lord Mulgrave, in 1835, was 'one of the great causes of alienation from the Government of the Irish people . . . We have party judges, we still have party sheriffs and of necessary consequence we must have partisan jurors'.[19] He went on to press the claims of his brother, John O'Connell, to the shrievalty in Kerry. Mulgrave was sympathetic to this argument but Russell, the home secretary, was more circumspect. While accepting that action was necessary to redress the balance in favour of catholics where official appointments were concerned, he was anxious that Mulgrave should not go too far in this direction. In the appointment of sheriffs he ruled that Mulgrave was not bound to select the first name on the list, but he should not ignore the list altogether unless all those named were incapable or unqualified, or there had been a clear attempt to force his choice by naming only one genuine candidate. John O'Connell would have to wait until the next year.[20]

During Mulgrave's administration, there was a deliberate attempt to appoint to public offices men who would not be regarded as hostile to the catholic community. This policy was fiercely opposed by many prominent protestants who believed it amounted to undue political interference. Speaking in the house of lords in 1836, the Earl of Winchilsea presented a petition from Francis Leigh protesting against the cancellation of his appointment as sheriff of Wexford the previous year. Winchilsea objected both to the fact that the judge's list had been passed over and to the grounds on which Leigh's appointment had allegedly been cancelled, his association with Orange societies. Mulgrave defended his right to ignore the judge's list, citing a precedent from 1830 when the Duke of Northumberland had passed over a Catholic, Mr Lyons, nominated for Kerry. Mulgrave stated three objections to Leigh: he was believed to be the master of an Orange lodge, he was a strong political partisan and he had no property in the county. He later admitted, however, that since the information concerning Leigh's memebership of an Orange society appeared to be erroneous, he was perfectly eligible for the situation of sheriff.[21] Further protest was caused by Mulgrave's return to the old practice of consulting out-going sheriffs on their successors. The chief baron, Henry Joy, was moved to send a letter of protest to the undersecretary, Thomas Drummond, pointing out that Peel had taken the right of nomination away from sheriffs because they were felt to be too susceptible to local influence. Drummond blithely dismissed Joy's complaint, observing that the government was merely returning to ancient usage and that in the opinion of the lord lieutenant sheriffs could provide the best local information.[22] Later governments seem to have returned the nomination to the judges. A special report on local government in Ireland, prepared for the select committee on local government and taxation in 1878, noted that high sheriffs were appointed by the lord lieutenant from a list of three names submitted by the judge of assize.[23]

Routine duties were delegated to the sub-sheriff but certain matters required the attention of the sheriff himself. County meetings, for example, which were a frequent recourse in times of disturbance, were convened by the sheriff and he was expected to attend in person. Thus in August 1829 we find the high sheriff of Tipperary, Matthew Jacob, convening a county meeting in Clonmel to discuss the disordered state of Tipperary, at which, he later acquainted the chief secretary, it was agreed that the county would provide £700 towards the expense of two stipendiary magistrates.[24] Jacob was also in the chair of a subsequent meeting of seventy-five magistrates in Thurles which passed resolutions calling for the introduction of the insurrection act and an increase in military posts.[25] As the returning officer for the county, the sheriff was responsible for the preservation of the peace during parliamentary elections. Contested elections could all too easily degenerate into party riots and as soon as an election was called urgent requests were sent out by sheriffs and their deputies for troops and police to be stationed at polling places. In January 1835 the high sheriff of Mayo, J.N. Gildea, apprised the under secretary, William Gosset, that:

> in consequence of the *many* attacks made at the former election, to obstruct freeholders from coming to the poll, and apprehending such attempts *more frequently* at the coming election, I consider it advisable to apply to government for a *strong* military force.

> Three troops of cavalry, and five of infantry, together with he police, will not, in my opinion, exceed that which may be required to protect freeholders, and keep the peace.[26]

Similar requests came in from all over the country, placing a considerable strain on the forces of law and order. One historian has estimated that about two-thirds of the total military force in Ireland in 1835 was employed on election duty, and this proportion increased in later years. During the election of 1868 almost every military detachment in the country was occupied on election duty of some kind.[27] The problem for government was to balance the demands for additional force with the need to prevent the army and the constabulary being over-stretched. Faced with just this problem in 1872, the under secretary, Thomas Burke, sought the advice of his long-serving predecessor, Thomas Larcom. The high sheriff of Galway, Burke explained, appeared 'to have lost his wits and is asking us to move a regular army into Galway'. Larcom replied that sheriffs' requisitions had always been a 'troublesome business' with which to deal. The sheriff was responsible for the peace of the county and was obliged to be present at elections. He was, therefore, entitled to the full support of government forces to the extent that they could be supplied without inconvenience to other requirements. He recommended that there should always be more rather than less force available than might be required in an emergency, advocating a strong detachment at each polling place and sufficient extra force for escorts and other duties. He also advised Burke to contact the local police inspector and resident magistrate for their assessment of the situation. [28]

In addition to providing for the preservation of the peace, the sheriff was responsible for erecting polling booths and making all the necessary arrangements for the holding of an election. The manner in which the sheriff executed his duties could have a significant influence on the conduct of an election. Reporting on the election in Limerick city in 1847, the *Limerick Chronicle* was full of praise for the performance of the sheriff, Richard Russell.

> The High Sheriff and his efficient assistant, Dr Gelston, were on the ground constantly from eight in the morning, when the polling commenced, actively directing, superintending and carrying out all the very excellent arrangements, which had emanated from the High Sheriff, and, as the issue told, were crowned with the happiest success . . . never, we repeat, having observed an election in Limerick pass over, and the entire proceedings in one day conclude, with such order, tranquillity and good humour on both sides. [29]

Before 1850 each county had only one polling place, but this was increased to between three and five by the franchise act of that year. In the early decades of the century polling took place over a number of days. Under the reform act of 1832 five days were allowed for Irish county elections. This was reduced to two days in 1850 and finally to one in 1862. Both nomination day and polling day were named by the sheriff, with polling booths being erected in the interval between the two. The sheriff's discretion in this regard was a matter of some political moment. Appearing before the select committee on parliamentary and municipal elections in 1869, James Spaight, who had been a

conservative candidate in Limerick City in 1865, described how sheriffs who had liberal or nationalist sympathies often arranged for nomination day to be on a Saturday and polling day the following Monday,
leaving the Sunday, traditionally a good day for the liberals, for can-
vassing, but 'if it should be in the opposite way, the sheriff knowing the
very great use that is made of the Sunday for that purpose generally
appoints it in the week days as it was at the last election'.[30]

Requisitions from sheriffs for military and police aid were not confined to election time. They and their deputies were authorised to requisition troops as escorts for judges, prisoners and witnesses to and
from the assizes if the local police force was judged inadequate for the
task, or if they anticipated resistance to the serving or executing of
civil process or decrees. In most cases it was the sub-sheriff who was
required to exercise this power. During the Land War when many
sub-sheriffs found themselves in the front line in the battle between
landlords and tenants, there was frequent recourse to police and military aid. In March 1880 the sub-sheriff of Roscommon (J. Hackett),
advised the under-secretary at the Castle of his unsuccessful attempt
to serve a number of ejectment decrees at Cloonturbet. He related
that he had found an excited mob of men, women and children in
front of the houses who refused to allow him possession, and that the
inside of one house appeared to be full of people stripped to the waist
and armed with scythes and pitchforks. Faced with this opposition
Hackett prudently retreated. In the thirty-four years in which he had
been sub-sheriff of Roscommon, he observed, he had never met with
opposition of this sort and until the last few months had very seldom
taken out police. He now requested the attendance of at least one
hundred police and a party of dragoons together with one or more
resident magistrates, urging that 'the sooner a powerful demonstra-
tion is made in support of the civil power, the more effect it will have'.
Hackett's request was granted and was, as he later reported, 'attended
with the best results'. Far from showing any opposition the tenants
apologised for what had happened on the previous occasion, where-
upon he took it upon himself to put them back on the land as care-
takers. By the beginning of 1882, applications for military parties to
protect sub-sheriffs serving writs or supervising the sale of distrained
goods became so numerous that the military authorities insisted that
sub-sheriffs requiring aid should be instructed to apply through R.I.C.
county inspectors detailing the exact spot where the military were to
meet the sheriff, the probable distance that would be travelled during
the day and the approximate number of days the party would be
required.[31]

Performance of the duties associated with the sheriff's office was
vital to the peace of the county and, while the office itself was often

little more than an honorary position, it could involve the active participation of the holder in the maintenance of law and order. At the beginning of the century sheriffs were drawn almost exclusively from the protestant landed community and although appointments of catholics increased in later decades, they remained under-represented in the shrievalty. By the end of the century it was an honour that few catholics sought, for in an increasingly polarised community it threatened to place the recipient in public opposition to the local population.

County Governors, Lords Lieutenant of Counties and Magistrates

The most senior civil offices in the county were largely honorific. The chief civil officer was the custos rotulorum (keeper of records) who was charged with custody of the county records and, up until the passage of the county courts act in 1877,[32] was responsible for the appointment of the clerk of the peace. He also administered the oath of office to the sub-sheriff. The office of custos rotulorum was usually held in conjunction with a county governorship. County governors were equivalent to lords lieutenant of counties in England, but unlike England where there was one lord lieutenant for each county, Irish counties often had more than one governor. Carlow and Cork had five each, Fermanagh and Meath four, and eight other counties three. In England the lord lieutenant acted as the senior magistrate in the county and served as a medium of communication between the local gentry and central government. In Ireland the multiplicity of governors presented ministers with a confusing division of responsibility as well as competing claims and representations, since one of the main functions of the governor was to nominate individuals for the post of deputy governor and for the commission of the peace. Governors were appointed for life and were almost invariably senior noblemen. Many were absentees. Some did take an active role in the affairs of their respective counties. Lord Caledon, who served as governor of Tyrone in the 1820s, was in regular correspondence with ministers concerning the state of the county. In 1828 he addressed himself to the chief secretary, Francis Leveson Gower, requesting advice as to the proper person to convene county meetings in the absence of Lord Belmore, who was both governor and custos rotulorum of Tyrone. Caledon was unsure whether the authority rested on the high sheriff or on Caledon himself as governor, or on both of them. His uncertainty was, he believed, symptomatic of a deeper problem:

> until this county is placed under the control of some individual visited with ample and acknowledged powers, it will continue to experience the inconvenience which arises from irregularity in the discharge of public duties and be ultimately exposed to serious injury.

In response the Castle law adviser, Richard Greene, observed that while it was the duty of the sheriff rather than the governor to convene county meetings, there was nothing to stop magistrates meeting and passing resolutions without being publicly convened. Caledon's suggestion that the county should be placed under the control of one individual was ignored.[33]

The proliferation of governors tended to reduce the importance of the office both in the eyes of its holders and of ministers, and the idea of appointing a chief governor was frequently mooted.[34] This was one of the first reforms discussed by the new administration, headed by Lord Anglesey, which assumed responsibility for Ireland after the whig victory in the general election of 1830.[35] Anglesey was anxious to change the existing system, which he described to the home secretary, Lord Melbourne, in January 1831, as being as bad as possible. 'There is no fixed person from whom inquiry upon general subjects may be sought. None from whom any knowledge may be obtained with respect to the character of magistrates, and the appointment of new ones.'[36] It was an article of faith with whig ministers that Irish magistrates were all too often unreliable, inefficient and politically disaffected. One of the aims of whig policy was to reduce the degree to which government was forced to rely on their intervention in local affairs. Replacing county governors by lords lieutenant would provide ministers with a recognised source of information and influence in each county and whereas the majority of governors were tory in their political sympathies the new lords lieutenant would owe their appointments if not their allegiance to the whigs. The idea was not to select a government supporter in every instance but to avoid those seen as political extremists. Anglesey believed that those appointed 'must be residents, influential, impartial, as far as it is possible to obtain them of that character in this unhappy land'.[37] The list of lords lieutenant of counties published in the *Dublin Gazette* in October 1831[38] contained a number of prominent Tories, including the Earl of Enniskillen (Fermanagh) and Lord Caledon (Tyrone), but omitted many others such as Lords Londonderry and Farnham, whose exclusion was attributed to party malice. But having created an office whose holder was to be in regular communication with ministers it was inevitable that the latter would appoint men on whom they felt they could rely.

Criticism of a different character came from O'Connell, who had opposed the bill creating lords lieutenant when it came before the commons in July, on the grounds that it would tend to create 'a little despotism' in every county and to secure the exclusion of catholics from the magistracy. Whilst admitting the unsatisfactory nature of the existing system, he argued that it did at least allow different representations from different governors which provided some security against improper appointments.[39] O'Connell's fears were to some extent justified. Responding to a protest from Lord Downshire in January 1832 that his representation concerning the appointment of a clerk of the crown for the north-eastern circuit had been ignored, Anglesey observed that Downshire seemed to believe that as lord lieutenant of County Down he could assume the whole patronage of the county. Whilst assuring him that he would try to meet his wishes, Anglesey warned that he would not always be able to do so.[40] Giving lords lieutenant a central role in the appointment of magistrates was also, as O'Connell feared, to prove a mixed blessing. Lords lieutenant did provide a valuable source of local information, reporting on the background and character of individuals proposed for the commission, but they also proved, in some cases, a major obstacle in the path of those seeking the appointment of catholic and/or liberal magistrates. Discontent on this issue amongst Irish MPs in 1835 prompted Mulgrave's chief secretary, Lord Morpeth, to take up the cases of two men, Mr Doolan and Mr Barron, who had been recommended for the commission in the King's County by the local (liberal) MPs, Nicholas FitzSimon and J.C. Westenra, but whose appointments had been blocked by the lord lieutenant of the King's County, Lord Oxmantown. Morpeth wrote to the lord chancellor about the matter[41] and discussed it with Oxmantown himself who insisted that the two men were not sufficiently qualified in either property or station in the county and that their appointments would on that account be distasteful to the other magistrates with whom they would have to act.[42] The issue was one which continued to provoke public criticism. A letter to the *Freeman's Journal* in 1869, from 'a county solicitor', complained that in far too many instances the commission was conferred by lieutenants of counties as

> a sort of honorary distinction on their friends or political partisans, without either party ever for a moment considering that the person appointed should, even for once in his life, attend to the discharge of the serious and responsible duties of the office. The result is that the courts of petty sessions have so frequently to be adjourned because of the non-attendance of even a single magistrate, to the great loss and disappointment of the suitors.[43]

The duties of lords lieutenant were not clearly defined. A printed circular from the chief secretary, Edward Stanley, addressed to all newly-appointed lords lieutenants in September 1831, referred to the office as entailing, 'rather by implication than expressly', functions of 'considerable delicacy'. These included providing names of suitable deputy lieutenants, conveying to the lord chancellor their opinion of the conduct and character of the magistracy and keeping themselves informed of political and local feeling in their counties, communicating to government such information as they might deem of importance. 'The officers of police', Stanley concluded,

> will be directed to furnish your lordship with periodical reports and they will in cases of urgency take your lordship's direction for their conduct. Upon such occasions, your lordship will of course lose no time in communicating with me for the information of the lord lieutenant.[44]

A similar circular from the under-secretary, issued to all deputy lieutenants the following year, directed that deputies should perform in their particular district the duties which the lord lieutenant performed for the county as a whole.

> These duties combine all matters connected with the due and vigorous execution of the law, the effectual preservation of the public peace, the conduct of magistrates and constables, in short everything pertaining to the good order, and government of the county, falls within the range of the deputy's functions and will justify and require his attention, as well with a view to his personal exertions, as to his communicating with his principal.[45]

The circular provoked much dissatisfaction among ordinary magistrates who resented the implication that deputy lieutenants had some control over their conduct. Apprising Gosset of the hostile reaction, Stanley warned him that magistrates were very jealous of their independence in relation to the lord lieutenant of the county, let alone his deputies. Lord lieutenants were recognised as being as the head of the county magistracy but they had no powers to appoint, remove or censure other magistrates.[46] Gosset's mistake was to put into words what had carefully been left vague in the earlier circular to lords lieutenant. The intention behind the latter's creation was to increase supervision of and ideally control over local magistrates but this could not be spelt out in an act of parliament or, indeed, a government circular.

It is difficult to generalise about levels of activity amongst lords lieutenant since, as was the case with other county officers, these varied according to inclination and opportunity. Many seem to have regarded the post as a sinecure and rarely communicated with government. Others took their position and responsibilities very seriously and carried on a regular correspondence with ministers. Lord Caledon, who was appointed lord lieutenant of Tyrone in 1831, is a prime example of the latter group. From the date of his appointment he busied himself with county affairs, keeping a copy of his correspondence in a special letter book. Shortly after his appointment in September 1831, he was writing to the local police superintendent, Major D'Arcy, to request a return of the number of police at the various stations in the county, considering it his duty as lord lieutenant 'to require such information upon every subject that may in any way be considered connected with that office'.[47] He made separate requests for returns of all the magistrates and yeomanry corps in the county.[48] Over the following years Caledon reported on the state of the county, both with regard to specific incidents, such as an arson attack on the national school-house at Ballygawley in 1835,[49] and more generally, on the conduct of local magistrates and of the police, and on other matters. In October 1835, for example, he notified Morpeth of a meeting that had been held in Dungannon to enquire into the delay in payments due to road contractors at the last assizes. (The county treasurer had apparently absconded with the grand jury funds.) The situation had worrying implications, Caledon observed, not only for the contractors, who were owed over £2,600, but also for the peace of the county. Any attempt to raise the money by another levy on cesspayers would, he feared, provoke the most extensive discontent. To avoid this, he requested a government loan to pay off the contractors and to meet ongoing expenses.[50] The government advanced money to maintain the county jail but was reluctant to take on the grand jury's debts, eventually offering a loan of £4,000 on the condition that the county would pledge itself to repay the sum by instalments and also to guarantee the payment of whatever balance was due by the defaulting treasurer.[51]

Implicit in the lord lieutenant's position as head of the magistracy was a supervisory function. In this role he acted as a kind of legal ombudsman, initiating investigations into cases of alleged misconduct by magistrates, or by the police. A case from County Cavan illustrates how this procedure worked. In July 1833, James Pogue petitioned Anglesey for redress in relation to his ill-treatment by members of the constabulary force in Cootehill the previous April. Pogue stated that he was a travelling salesman who had been moved on by a police constable, Crosby O'Reilly, when he attempted to erect a stand in Cootehill. When Pogue remonstrated, pointing out that he had been erecting his stand in the same place for twenty-five years, he was arrested and charged with assault. He had been verbally abused by the presiding magistrate, Mr Murphy, who initially refused him bail, keeping him in jail for two hours. The petition was referred by Anglesey to the lord lieutenant of Cavan, Lord Headford, who directed one of his deputy lieutenants, Major Burrows, to institute an inquiry. Burrows examined all the parties and concluded that O'Reilly was simply carrying out orders from the magistrates concerning road obstructions. Pogue, it was claimed, had given O'Reilly bad language and had been charged with obstructing the police in the execution of their duty, not with assault. Murphy was stated not to have acted in the manner claimed. Pogue was said to have been brought before the clerk of petty sessions and after informations had been taken against him, he was given bail, being released in less than one hour. On the basis of Burrows's report, Headfort concluded that the allegations had not been substantiated. The outcome of the investigation did not satisfy Pogue or his employer, Robert Galbraith, who wrote to Gosset in September complaining about Pogue's treatment and accusing the government of winking at misconduct by the police and of failing to take complaints seriously. Gosset rejected the charge, explaining coldly that the complaint had been investigated and that if Pogue still felt aggrieved he could pursue the matter through the courts.[52] Lords lieutenant appear to have become less central to the investigation of complaints later in the century as other bureaucratic procedures were introduced for this purpose. Rules drawn up for the guidance of the constabulary, following the consolidation of the force in 1836, laid down that complaints against the police should be investigated by magistrates in petty sessions, although in practice most cases were referred to the police themselves in the first instance.[53]

Despite the growing number of government functionaries in the Irish counties to whom ministers could refer, lords lieutenant were not entirely eclipsed and their opinions continued to carry weight. Their recommendations governed entry to the commission of the peace and in the event of disorder or disturbance they were consulted on the state of their respective counties. The lords lieutenant of counties Louth and Dublin, Lords Rathdonnell and Monck, were consulted in 1876, for example, on the advisability of revoking the proclamation of their counties under the peace preservation act, although Rathdonnell's contention that the quiet in County Louth was a result of the proclamation and would be threatened if it was removed, did not impress the chief secretary, Sir Michael Hicks-Beach, who remarked to the viceroy, Lord Abercorn, that he would attach more weight to Rathdonnell's opinion if he had made inquiries on the spot instead of writing from London.[54] Despite Hicks-Beach's reservations Louth was not released from the act, which was still in force some months later. Rathdonnell persisted in arguing for its retention, prompting Hicks-Beach to exclaim to Abercorn that he much inclined to request him to call a meeting of magistrates to gauge their opinion.[55] Individual lords lieutenant continued to see it as their duty to keep ministers informed of political feeling in the county. Shocked by the declaration in November 1880, by the newly elected MP for the borough of Wexford, Tim Healy, that he saw it as his mandate 'to give expression on every occasion and in every way to the undying spirit of hostility which animates us all to British domination in Ireland', Lord Carew thought it right as lord lieutenant of the county to send a report of the speech to the chief secretary, William Arnold Forster, adding that he regretted to say that the doctrines of the land league were spreading in the county.[56]

One of the reasons why protestant lords lieutenant of counties, and Protestant magistrates, objected to the appointment of catholics to the commission was their belief that they would act as political partisans. A magistrate from the Strabane bench, E.T. Herdman, complained to Lord Belmore, lord lieutenant of County Tyrone in 1895, that a good many catholics had been put onto the bench 'most of them of extreme political views and all inclined to combine to achieve[?] their own ends. They are all local and can be whipped up when required'. [57] To counteract this Herdman urged the appointment of at least three respectable protestant magistrates without delay. When Belmore suggested that the proposed appointments would themselves be partisan, Herdman argued that

> unless the superior type of Protestant magistrates have a certain amount of attendance and backing from their own class and creed they will cease attending the bench and the business will fall into the hands of the Home Rule faction greatly to the detriment of the public interest.

It was not only a question of the influence of the catholic magistrates at petty sessions, 'they flock in a body at quarter sessions and although they preach temperance they nearly always support any Roman catholic application for a special licence [to sell alcohol]'.[58] Although magistrates in quarter sessions did not exercise the same administrative powers that their counterparts in England had enjoyed prior to the local government act of 1888, Irish magistrates did acquire a direct role in local administration through their participation in presentment sessions, which examined applications for county funds prior to their presentation to the grand jury, and as ex officio members of poor law boards. The composition of the magistracy, which remained overwhelmingly protestant until the end of the century (the proportion of catholic magistrates which had stood at just over 10% in 1834, had only risen to 25% by 1886),[59] influenced popular perceptions not only of the administration of justice but also of that of poor relief. And while magistrates drawn from the protestant gentry might resent the influx of catholics to the commission, their presence on the bench was seen as essential if public confidence was to be maintained, a point which a group of catholic clergymen from County Down had urged on the lord lieutenant of the county, Lord Dufferin, in 1869. Attributing the want of confidence amongst catholics in the administration of justice and of the laws for the relief of the poor to the small number of catholic magistrates and ex officio guardians, they submitted that

in both these departments of the local management of affairs, the business
is too frequently transacted in a way prejudiced to the interests and feelings of Roman Catholics, who, we respectfully submit are entitled to a
more adequate representation in those quarters.[60]

Presbyterians in the northern counties were equally sensitive to the
religious imbalance amongst magistrates. Residents of Sixmilecross in
County Tyrone, petitioned Lord Belmore in 1892 for an increase in
the local magistracy arguing that two of the leading religious denominations, Church of Ireland and Roman Catholic, were already represented on the magisterial bench but no local presbyterian as yet held
office, 'notwithstanding the fact that a very large number of the inhabitants of the district belong to the denomination'.[61] To a greater or
lesser extent, depending on local circumstances, magistrates were
expected to act as representatives of their particular communities and
it was against this background that the intrusion of politics into magisterial business must be understood.

Ministerial dissatisfaction with the conduct of ordinary magistrates,
as well as problems caused by their uneven distribution across the
country, resulted in the appointment of stipendaries. Such appointments had been made on an ad hoc basis from the early years of the
century but they did not become a regular feature of rural life until
mid-century. The decisive shift from deploying stipendaries as a temporary expedient to their general employment across the country
took place in the 1830s as part of the efforts of whig ministers to establish a legal bureaucracy which was not vitiated by sectarian divisions.
The number of stipendaries rose from eleven in 1831 to fifty-four in
1839 and continued to increase, reaching a total of seventy-three in
1860.[62] It remained at around this figure for the remainder of the century. Appointments were made by the viceroy and the exercise of government patronage became a regular focus for opposition criticism.
Unlike appointments of assistant barristers and crown prosecutors,
which were restricted to legally qualified candidates, stipendiary magistrates needed no particular qualifications and ministers found themselves under great pressure to appoint individuals referred to them by
their parliamentary supporters. Most of the eighteen stipendaries
appointed following the reorganisation of the constabulary in 1836,
were political recommendations and, while none was positively unfit,
ministers felt sufficiently uneasy in the face of continued attacks on
their qualifications to lay down regulations governing the selection of
future candidates. Appearing before a house of lords select committee in 1839, the undersecretary, Thomas Drummond, stated that the
government had introduced a rule that no-one should be appointed as
a stipendiary magistrate who had not previously acted as a magistrate,
or been educated for the bar, or had served in the constabulary, and

that every appointment should be subject to an examination by the attorney general.[63] Stipendiary or, as they increasingly became known, resident magistrates continued to attract criticism on grounds of inefficiency and political partiality, but, whilst recognising the problems inherent in the system, ministers found it too valuable to dispense with. In a memorandum drawn up in response to reservations voiced by the chief secretary, Sir Robert Peel, in 1862, Thomas Larcom acknowledged that ordinary magistrates resented the presence of stipendiaries but pointed out that the former were

> glad to throw on the paid magistrate (and consider that they have a right to do so) the unpleasant duties which the state of Ireland requires, such as attendance with the police at riots, races, fairs, faction fights, and meetings of all kinds, quelling disturbances and night work. At elections, for example, they [i.e. ordinary magistrates] for the most part abstain from acting and very properly so, for their personal sympathies are necessarily in this angry country with one side or the other. No-one but a public officer is neutral in Ireland and everyone else, however really impartial, is always supposed by the people to lean one way. They like the dignity of presiding at the bench and too many covet the commission for the name and status which it gives and for the ex-officio seat at the poor house board, with a vote for the union appointments, who can hardly be got to attend the bench at all. This no doubt is unwholesome but inevitable so long as the present state of things continues.

The real problem, Larcom hinted, was appointing resident magistrates from the 'county gentlemen' who were 'the least useful generally speaking but the most pressed by MPs'.[64] The extent to which resident magistrates were regarded by the people as 'independent of their local feelings and disputes' was always questionable and became increasingly so in the 1880s and 1890s when they were branded as servants of a hostile government.

Local Government in Rural Areas
B. The Grand Jury

Despite the survival of grand jury records dating back to the eighteenth century and beyond, no comprehensive study of the administrative work of these bodies has appeared.[65] In the early nineteenth century the grand jury was the most important local body in rural Ireland, empowered to raise money by means of county rates for a variety of purposes from the construction and repair of roads and bridges to the upkeep of the local institutions such as hospitals and lunatic asylums. It was also the most heavily criticised. Politicians, pamphleteers and novelists all regaled the public with tales of grand jury abuses while cess-payers complained of inefficiency and extravagance. The system was subject to parliamentary investigation on numerous occasions and ministers were united in regarding it as unsatisfactory. A series of reforms culminating in the grand jury act of 1836, regulated proceedings and gave cess-payers a limited role in deciding how local taxes should be spent, but the system never entirely shook off its reputation for corruption and partiality. The limited nature of grand jury reform should not, however, disguise its importance as a political issue. For it was one which went to the heart of Irish politics in the pre-Famine period, embracing matters of taxation and expenditure, landlord and tenant relations, political and religious exclusivity and the divergence between English and Irish experience. Different groups approached the question with different agenda. Local landowners were concerned to preserve their own influence over local affairs, and particularly over local expenditure, catholic politicians wished to break the monopoly of power long enjoyed by members of the protestant ascendancy and cess-payers were anxious to reduce a growing financial burden.

The main task of the grand jury, as far as fiscal business was concerned, was the consideration of presentments for the construction and maintenance of roads and bridges, and this constituted the major part of grand jury discussions. Statutes passed in the eighteenth and early nineteenth centuries considerably extended the potential range of grand jury activities. In 1708, for example, juries were given the power to levy money for the building and repair of sessions houses and gaols and in 1739 to pay the salaries of a parish watch.[66] Towards the end of the eighteenth century grand juries were authorised to take limited measures to provide for the social welfare of the local population. From 1765 they could make contributions towards the cost of establishing a county infirmary as an inducement to subscribers to make up the deficiency in the amount required to maintain a hospital, and a few years later an act providing for the erection and maintenance of houses of industry (workhouses) empowered grand juries to levy a portion of the costs on the county.[67] In the early nineteenth century dispensaries could be provided on a similar basis, with grand juries granting sums equal to amounts raised by private subscription.[68] These statutes were enabling rather than prescriptive – only nine counties adopted the act providing for the erection of houses of industry, for example[69] – and as concern about social conditions grew an element of compulsion began to creep into legislation. Provision for the lunatic poor is a case in point. In 1806 grand juries were authorised to add wards to existing houses of industry for the treatment of lunatics and to present a sum for the purpose not exceeding £100 p.a. Since there were few houses of industry this act had little effect and in 1817 the first of a series of measures was passed to enable the government to build district lunatic asylums and to appoint boards of governors to manage them, the cost being levied on the counties.[70] Nine such asylums catering for 980 patients were opened between 1825 and 1835 at a cost of nearly £210,000.[71] From 1822 central government also took over administrative, though not fiscal, responsibility for policing the counties. Thus while the grand jury represented the primary organ of local government in the Irish counties its function was increasingly that of a taxing rather than an administrative authority.

In his *Account of Ireland, Statistical and Political*, published in 1812, the English writer Edward Wakefield described the Irish grand jury as 'a sort of county parliament, in which numbers are anxious to have a seat'.[72] Grand jurors certainly believed that their collective opinion was of consequence and the passing of resolutions on political issues was a common feature of their proceedings. At the spring assizes of 1807 the grand jury of County Tyrone entered into a unanimous resolution against catholic claims, which the county MPs were instructed to oppose. (A similar resolution had already been passed in Fermanagh.)[73] Some years later Tyrone jurors approved a resolution 'viewing with disgust the proceedings of the Catholic Board' and 'trusting that the wisdom of the legislature will put down all factions without encroaching on the right of petition'.[74] Reaching agreement on political questions was not always straightforward however. Efforts to persuade the grand jury of County Limerick to pass a resolution in favour of the union in 1831 were only successful when a second resolution supporting parliamentary reform was also approved.[75]

One indication of the growth in power and influence of grand juries from the late eighteenth century is provided by the increasing attention paid to the design of court and sessions houses. Jurors were often prepared to devote considerable time and expense to providing themselves with surroundings which they felt suitably reflected their importance. A particularly well-documented case concerns the endeavours of the grand jurors of County Louth to build themselves a new court house in Dundalk. Having decided on the need for a new building, the grand jury appointed a committee in 1810 to contract with an architect and supervise the work. This task was considerably complicated by the discovery in April 1812 that the grand jury had no legal power to contract with one person for the whole project. Later that year, having pulled down the old court house and laid out foundations, the architect resigned, objecting to the committee's intention of appointing craftsmen to undertake the work instead of leaving this to him as originally agreed. By the end of September work was at a standstill.[76] The jurors seem to have been rescued by an act of parliament passed in 1813,[77] which enabled grand juries to appoint overseers empowered to make contracts for the building of court houses and sessions houses to be approved by the grand jury. The new courthouse was eventually completed, but its design, which was based on Greek classical architecture, does not appear to have met with universal approval. The building was to be described by Richard Lalor Sheil as 'the most beautiful and inconvenient temple in which the rites of justice have ever been performed'.[78]

Members of the grand jury were selected by the high sheriff from the leading property owners in the county, the order in which the jurors stood on the list being an indication of their social standing. The sheriff's discretion in the nomination of the grand jury was total, although his choice was sometimes limited by a poor attendance at the assizes. The Marquis of Abercorn's agent, James Hamilton, reported from the Lifford assizes in 1804 that the sheriff of County Tyrone had been obliged to put persons onto the jury 'little above the rank of common farmers'.[79] The sheriff was generally a political appointment and it frequently happened that he filled the list with his friends and supporters. Giving evidence to a commons select committee on grand jury presentments in 1815, the whig MP for the Queen's County, Sir Henry Parnell, observed that

> the practice in Ireland is, for the lord lieutenant to appoint sheriffs of counties by communication with those members of parliament who generally support government; the sheriffs frequently form their panels of the counties in communication with those members; and the consequence is, a considerable degree of improper influence in the actual formation of many grand juries'.[80]

Membership of the grand jury carried considerable honorific value and the order of precedence was taken very seriously. A Sligo landowner, John Knox, wrote indignantly to the Marquess of Sligo in 1832 that he had been placed forty-fourth on the grand jury panel although his property in the county entitled him to a much higher place. While he had been a political opponent of Sligo's relative, the late Denis Browne, it was, he conceded,

> quite consistent that those who approved of [Browne's] politics, should seek to *depreciate* an influence opposed to them. I was *therefore* called on the panel in the lowest place they could think of. I still answered to my name, *however low on the panel I might be called*, and was *then* left off entirely.

So long as his place on the panel was a political matter, Knox's personal influence was not badly damaged, since if political hostility dictated his place 'it also at the same time *accounted for it*, but, if I were *now* to submit to be called thus *ridiculously out of my place*, the public would naturally come to believe that to be the only place to which I was entitled.'[81]

Catholics were prohibited from serving on grand juries until 1793 and even after this date jury lists were predominantly, though not exclusively, protestant, the result partly of political and religious discrimination and partly of the concentration of property in protestant hands. Analysis of the composition of the grand jury of County Cork in the period from 1836 to 1899 has shown that the majority of jurors came from a small, inter-linked group of landed families.[82] Members of prominent catholic families did serve as grand jurors in certain counties (Daniel O'Connell's brothers, John and James, were placed on the grand jury list in Kerry in the 1820s for example) but this was not typical of the country as a whole. Controversy over the composition of grand juries was not confined to the personal or political bias of the sheriff. There was also the vexed question of the non-representation of cess-payers. County cess was levied on occupiers, not owners, of land. As grand jurors were, by definition, property owners the men raising and expending cess were taxing not themselves but their tenants. This, as was frequently pointed out, offended against the principle of no taxation without representation. To make matters worse grand jurors acquired an unsavoury reputation for corruption. The presentment system was wide open to abuse. Anyone wishing to make or repair a road simply drew up a certificate stating the necessity of the work and the estimated cost, attested by two persons before a justice of the peace, and submitted this to the grand jury at the assizes. Pressure of business was sometimes so great that grand jurors were able to devote just a few minutes to the consideration of each presentment. The select committee on grand jury presentments which sat in 1827 found that the grand jury of County Cork granted an average of seventy-five presentments a day during a ten-day assizes while that of County Down, which sat for four days, granted over 200 presentments each day.[83] Given this situation it was inevitable that the fate of an application depended more on the influence of the sponsor than on the merits of the case. At the beginning of the century there were few fixed landmarks or accurate maps, and little if any check was made on work performed, with the result that double or treble presentments were sometimes made for the same piece of road, or even for non-existent pieces of road. Writing from Dublin in 1818, Arthur Hutchins informed the chief secretary, Robert Peel, that one-sixth of the sums raised for public works were not expended on the object for which they were granted and cited examples from Cork and Kerry of roads presented for that were never built.[84] Others alleged that landlords obtained contracts for their tenants, who were then enabled to pay their rent out of public money.[85] An article in *The Metropolitan* in 1832 maintained that there was ample evidence that 'what are denominated public works in Ireland are in fact private speculations'.[86] The most common complaint was that grand jurors were only interested in the upkeep of their own neighbourhoods. Speaking in the commons in 1833, Lord Clements, who represented County Leitrim, stated that roads in Leitrim were impassable except in those parts where grand jurors resided.[87]

Major landowners relied on friends and allies, and on their agents, to protect their interests on grand juries. In the early decades of the nineteenth century matters relating to the Donegal and Tyrone estates of the Marquis of Abercorn, for example, were looked after by John Stewart, his unofficial political manager, together with his agent James Hamilton and Hamilton's successor, John James Burgoyne. In February 1807, Hamilton apprised Abercorn that he had applied for money for a road in the Baronscourt estate at the forthcoming spring assizes at Omagh, pointing out that Abercorn's tenants would thereby having the advantage both of the road itself and the money for making it. He also suggested that Abercorn should write to the neighbouring landowner, Lord Mountjoy, to ensure that his agent, Mr Chambers, was directed to co-operate with Hamilton in endeavouring to obtain presentments for the barony as a whole. 'Attending the assizes', Hamilton complained, 'has always been a most irksome part of my duty'.[88] An agency to a large estate did not automatically entitle the holder to a seat on the grand jury. John James Burgoyne found himself excluded from a grand jury in Donegal in 1810 as his name appeared on the panel too low down for him to be sworn in. Burgoyne protested indignantly to the sheriff, as he later reported to his employer, that it was 'most extraordinary [conduct] to put people on the jury who had comparatively nothing to represent and leave your Lordship's estate unrepresented.'[89]

At the root of the growing unease at the conduct of grand juries, manifest in the hours which MPs devoted to debating the issue both on the floor of the house and in committee rooms, lay the belief that landowners were setting the worst kind of example, encouraging perjury and immorality among the lower classes, and undermining the moral framework of society as a whole. In a pamphlet tellingly entitled, *An inquiry into the effect of the Irish grand jury laws, as affecting the industry, the improvement, and the moral character of the people of England*, published in 1815, Thomas Rice argued that under the existing state of the grand jury laws

> public burdens have augmented in a most formidable progression; the public works have become deteriorated in a similar ratio. The landlord is lowered in the general estimation by his acquiescence in a corrupt system; the peasant is impoverished and the community plundered . . . If education, independence, a dread of public reprobation, and religious principle, do not control the magistrate, how is the peasant, ignorant and impoverished, to be restrained?[90]

The impression that presentments were obtained through favouritism was felt to lessen public confidence not just in the civil and criminal business of the grand jury, but in the legal system as a whole. Writing to the lord lieutenant, Lord Anglesey, in 1832, Henry Lambert, MP for County Wexford, insisted that so long as grand juries were composed of political partisans, 'justice will be poisoned in its very source and people will turn in despair from the tainted tribunals of law and endeavour to redress their grievances by appeal to force'. Lambert's outburst was provoked by the action of the grand jury of County Wexford in passing a presentment for £18 in compensation for corn destroyed in a fire. Such presentments, which could be passed in compensation for malicious damage to property, were intended to have a deterrent effect but were often exploited for personal or political advantage. In this instance the fire was assumed to be malicious since the owner of the corn, George Gifford, acted as the agent of the local rector. Gifford applied to the grand jury to have the amount of his loss levied by presentment, but instead of levying the sum on the parish in which the outrage occurred, the grand jury had singled out a different parish every acre of which belonged to Lambert. Lambert maintained that his tenants had been penalised because his political opinions differed from those of some of the grand jurors. If the tranquillity of the county was to be preserved, it was of the utmost importance, he exhorted Anglesey, that the people should be convinced that 'injustice shall not be inflicted on them for the gratification of party revenge or the protection of party delinquents'.[91]

The pernicious effect of misconduct on the part of local bodies provides a sub-text to a number of early nineteenth-century novels whose action takes place in rural Ireland. Both Maria Edgeworth's *The Absentee* and William Carleton's *Valentine M'Clutchy*, for example, highlight the evils of absenteeism. Both feature a young man visiting his estate in disguise and discovering nothing but mismanagement and misery, and in each case the requisite happy ending sees the hero returning to live on the estate. In these novels abuses perpetrated by the grand jury are used to illustrate the mismanagement that occurs in the absence of 'rael jantlemen', to borrow Maria Edgeworth's phrase. Edgeworth's hero, for example, is informed that the roads in the neighbourhood of his estate are in a very bad condition,

> on account of there being no jantleman resident in it, nor near; but only a bit of an under-agent, a great little rogue, who gets his own turn out of the roads, and everything else in life. . . . the agent gets them a presentment for making so many perches of road from the grand jury, at twice the price that would make the road. And tenants are, by this means, as they take the road by contract, at the price given by the county, able to pay back all they get by the job, over and above potatoes and salt, back again to the agent, for the arrear on the land . . .

> And sure they'd never be got made at all, if they weren't made this ways . . . And when the rael jantlemen's resident in the country, there's no jobbing can be, because they're the leading men on the grand jury; and these journeymen jantlemen are then kept in order, and all's right.[92]

Carleton's *Valentine M'Clutchy*, written thirty years after *The Abstentee* but purporting to represent his native Ulster in 1804, presents a similar picture. One passage vividly recreates the scene in a grand jury room.

> We pass now to the grand jury room of the county, and truly as a subordinate tribunal for aiding the administration of justice, it was at the time of which we write, one of the most anomalous exhibitions that could be witnessed . . .

> It was a long room, about thirty-six or forty feet in length, by thirty, with a fire-place at each end, and one or two at the sides. Above the chimney-piece was an oil painting of William the Third, together with a small bronze of George the Third. There were some other portraits of past and present jurors, presented by themselves or their friends . . . Seated about a long table covered with green baize, were a number of men, with papers before them; whilst grouped in different parts of the room were the younger persons, amusing themselves by the accidents at the last meet – if it happened to be the hunting season – or the last duel, or the last female victim to the corruption and profligacy of some of those from whom the people were to expect justice, and their families protection.

During the course of the proceedings one juryman applies for a presentment for a bridge reminding his fellows that,

"Our party voted about thirty miles of roads to repair *thoroughly* and you know that although you only *veneered* them, we said nothing." "But," replied Val, "who ever heard of a bridge without water; and I know there's not a stream within three miles of you."

"Never mind that," replied M'Small, "let me have the bridge first, and we'll see what can be done about the water afterwards. If God in his mercy would send a wet winter next season, who knows but we might present for a new river at January assizes."

"You must have it," said Deaker, "give M'Small the bridge, and, as he says, we'll see afterwards what can be done for a river for it." The bridge was not only passed, but built, and actually stands to this day, an undeniable monument of the frugality and honesty of grand jurors, and the affection with which they were then capable of bearing to each other, when their interests happened to be at stake, which was just four times in the year.

In the meantime the tumultuous battle of jobs, in all its noise, recrimination, and jangle of conflicting interests, and incredible selfishness commenced. There were strong mutual objections to pass the roads to Mr Lucre and M'Clutchy, and a regular confict between the respective partisans accordingly took place.[93]

Neither Edgeworth nor Carleton was presenting a factual report of grand jury proceedings but their descriptions probably give a fairly accurate flavour of how some grand juries operated. Caricatures are, after all, only effective if they contain a recognisable element of the truth. Such accounts helped to reinforce an impression of incompetence and corruption in the conduct of grand jury affairs which was profoundly influential and which gave added weight to the campaign for reform. And it is clear that in some cases reality was not far removed from fiction. When one Tyrone grand juror attempted to raise the matter of irregularities in the construction of a new mail coach road at Omagh assizes in 1814, he was received with what he later described as 'contempt and indifference' and was informed that it was impertinent to interfere with roads leading through the estates of the Marquis of Abercorn and Lord Mountjoy.[94] But this was not the whole picture. A number of grand juries seem to have conducted themselves with reasonable efficiency and propriety. The grand jury of County Antrim, for example, took steps to tighten up procedures by which presentments were made and accounting affidavits approved in the first decade of the nineteenth century, some years before parliament addressed itself to the matter.[95] The problem, according to defenders of the system, was that the abuses perpetrated by some grand juries were being used to condemn them all. Reform was quite unnecessary in counties such as Louth, John Leslie Foster assured his uncle and former MP for the county, John Foster, in 1818, but I confess I cannot come to the same conclusion with respect to Tipperary, Limerick, Galway, Clare, Roscommon and some others. The impression is universal that some effective check must be put to the profusion of their expenditure and some security attained that the objects on which it is laid out should be such as an impartial man of sense would say deserved a preference. The misfortune of the case is that the impression taken up with respect to the whole system has been derived from the consideration of the worst parts of it.[96]

The growing dissatisfaction with the grand jury system in the early nineteenth century was made up of a number of different strands. There was resentment at the level of county taxation and at the unequal assessment based on out-dated valuation, there was frustration with the display of political and sectarian partiality and there was embarrassment at the level of corruption and inefficiency. A major difficulty facing would-be reformers was that the great body of Irish MPs had an interest in maintaining the system as it was, since they were amongst the beneficiaries of it. It is notable that many of the most vocal advocates of reform amongst Irish MPs were whigs who found themselves excluded from power in their localities. Sir John Newport informed the 1815 commons select committee on grand jury presentments that he had been excluded from the grand jury of the City of Limerick for almost seven years, despite being MP for the city, until the assize judge threatened to fine the sheriff.[97] Others such as Sir Henry Parnell, who represented the Queen's County, and Maurice Fitzgerald (County Kerry), had similar reasons for wishing to see a change in the system. Reform proposals, if they were to stand any chance of success, had to be limited to reducing the opportunity for abuse rather than introducing any fundamental change. Maurice Fitzgerald, who had prepared a bill to improve the method of accounting for money expended by grand juries in 1810, explained to the 1815 committee that he abandoned ideas of more radical reform after consulting with his fellow MPs and finding them resolved to retain the power of presenting money in grand juries, a power which Fitzgerald had wanted transferred to county magistrates.[98]

That a number of reforming measures did reach the statute books in the early decades of the century testifies to the persistence and determination of a small number of Irish members and demonstrates the vital role of the backbench MPs in initiating legislation. One of the moving spirits behind grand jury reform in this period was the MP for Sligo County, Edward Synge Cooper. In 1812 Cooper introduced a bill to tighten up the accounting procedures of grand juries. Although the bill passed both houses of parliament it was lost on its return to the commons from the lords, where it had been slightly amended. The loss of the bill prompted the intervention of William Vesey Fitzgerald, MP for Ennis and a member of the government, who publicly pledged himself to reform the system of grand jury taxation.[99] Fitzgerald was to come to regret this pledge. Would-be reformers bombarded him with advice and suggestions but, as he confessed to a fellow MP, Windham Wyndham-Quin, in January 1814, the matter was proving more difficult than he had imagined, and would occupy even more time than he had feared.[100] It was not until three years later that Fitzgerald finally presented a bill to the commons. This was strictly limited in scope, conferring on magistrates at quarter sessions a power to examine presentments prior to their consideration by the grand jury, but leaving the final decision on whether or not to allow a presentment to grand jurors themselves, and providing for the appointment of a civil engineer in each county to regulate and inspect public works.[101] The bill received an unenthusiastic reception, with some MPs regretting that it did not go further while others claimed it would lead to even higher local taxes. Sir George Hill, MP for Londonderry city, opposed the measure 'as being calculated to deprive the gentlemen of the country of their proper influence and authority and to transfer it to the county surveyors'.[102] By the time the bill became law in July,[103] it was clear that hostility to the creation of county surveyors was not confined to MPs. Lord Abercorn's agent, John James Burgoyne, observed to his employer that he could see no possible use that the act would answer. It would create 'a number of useless placemen whose emoluments would be more advantageously laid out on public works'. He had, nevertheless, already suggested that Abercorn might like to apply for the nomination of the surveyors of Counties Tyrone and Donegal.[104]

When it became apparent that there were serious flaws in the drafting of the act, opponents of the measure seized the opportunity to press for radical amendments.[105] Despite Fitzgerald's protestations that he would be made to look ridiculous, he was obliged to suspend the act in February 1818 and to introduce a new bill a few months later.[106] This omitted the clauses concerning the appointment of county surveyors as well as provisions which had restricted the consideration of presentments to the summer assizes. The bill passed without opposition. Welcoming the new act,[107] the *Dublin Evening Post* regretted that it had not done more for ordinary people, but professed itself pleased with what had been done. It described the act as 'the first stroke of an axe which will in time lop off the noxious and useless branches of this upas tree'.[108] *The Post* was correct in thinking that the process of reform was only just begun but it was to be many years before major surgery would be undertaken.

Pressure for grand jury reform continued to be exerted from the back benches throughout the 1820s. Select committees considered the issue in 1819, 1822 and 1827 and their reports led to further legislation, including an act providing for the payment of county officers by annual salaries according to a fixed scale and the establishment of a new land survey to provide the basis for uniform assessment of county cess.[109] With the appointment of the whig peer and Irish landowner, the Marquis of Lansdowne, as home secretary in July 1827, and Thomas Spring Rice as his undersecretary, it looked as though grand jury reform might be taken up by government. In August Lansdowne notified the Irish chief secretary, William Lamb, that he had been considering various suggestions for the improvement of local administration in Ireland, including grand jury reform.[110] Lamb was unenthusiastic about the prospect of legislating on the matter, warning that those measures which were most loudly demanded were often the most difficult to adopt.[111] The whigs lost office shortly afterwards but the possibility of introducing some measure of reform was broached by Lamb's successor, Francis Leveson Gower, in a letter to the new home secretary, Robert Peel, in 1828.[112] Peel advised caution: 'Of course every writer on Irish affairs calls for a reform of the grand jury laws but in this as in many other cases, the danger is that while you stop one hole, you make two'.[113] The real problem, as Peel recognised, was one which went to the heart of local administration in Ireland. If power was to remain in the localities was there any practicable alternative to the grand jury as the administrative body? 'To take the business into the hands of Government', Peel felt, 'is to widen the distinction between England and Ireland and to postpone the period at which local affairs in Ireland can be satisfactorily managed by local authorities'.[114] At Peel's suggestion Gower canvassed opinion on the advisability of reform but he came to no firm conclusion before leaving office in 1830, although he did tentatively suggest the admission of cess payers who held freeholds to the value of £50 p.a. to sit alongside magistrates at road sessions, believing that they could in some counties operate as a check on the 'selfish views of the county gentlemen'.[115] Peel agreed that the latter should be prevented from abusing their power but warned that they must be careful not to open the door to 'provincial demagogues' who would 'labour to inflame the mind of the people against the grand jury and to annoy and disgust the jurors'. Reform, in Peel's opinion, should be confined to improving the working of the existing system, which did at least stimulate wealthy proprietors and their heirs to some degree of exertion and relieved the executive government from multifarious duties

> which must devolve upon it if we were to act on the principle that local authorities cannot be trusted with the management of the county purse and that the Castle or boards appointed by the Castle, must undertake those duties which are now performed by the magistracy and by the parishes in England, and in Ireland by the grand jury.[116]

Peel's concern about 'provincial demagogues' who would take advantage of any concessions made to cess payers to give them a say in the expenditure of their money was no doubt heightened by the recent passage of catholic emancipation and the vocal demands of catholic leaders, such as O'Connell, for further reform to end the protestant monopoly of power. From this time on, the campaign for grand jury reform acquired a new character. In the first two decades of the century the issue was one which was taken up by Irish MPs, whose perspective was that of grand jurors rather than cess-payers. In the 1830s it became part of the package of reforms advocated not only by O'Connellite radicals but also by British and Irish whigs anxious to do 'justice to Ireland'. But whereas O'Connell called for an end to the system of grand jury administration and the introduction of a new system of county taxation based on the principle of local elections, the whigs baulked at direct representation of tax-payers. Work on a new measure of grand jury reform was under way soon after the whigs took office in November 1830.[117] The proposals were made public in the form of a bill published in October 1831,[118] which would repeal all previous acts and enact new provisions in their place. Under the bill, only those presentments approved by magistrates assembled at special road sessions were to be sent before the grand jury. All presentments granted by the grand jury were to be executed by contracts made on sealed tenders, and the lord lieutenant was empowered to appoint a qualified surveyor for such counties as he should think fit. From the passing of the bill, tenants were to deduct grand jury cess from their rent and all leases made thereafter at rack rents were to be free of cess. Ministers were determined to proceed cautiously and to consult widely before bringing the measure before the commons.

When the bill finally came up for discussion in February 1833 it had undergone a number of changes, the most significant of which were the opening of roads sessions to all magistrates irrespective of the value of their property and the co-option of a limited number of cess-payers to sit alongside magistrates. Introducing the measure the chief secretary, Edward Stanley, drew attention to the defects which vitiated grand jury administration. The grand jury, he observed, was not a responsible body, it was not subject to public opinion since its deliberations were carried on in private, and it had insufficient time to perform its functions efficiently. As far as remedies were concerned, Stanley maintained that major changes would not be beneficial and would not meet with the concurrence of Irish MPs. To introduce the principle of elections would, he believed, lead to 'corruption, confusion and irritation'. Instead, he proposed to ensure a more general representation of the various parts of the counties by making it mandatory on the high sheriff to put at least one juror from each barony on the grand jury and by providing for the selection of a certain number of the highest rate-payers to sit on baronial sessions.[119] Irish MPs were divided in their response. O'Connell claimed that Stanley had underestimated the evils of the existing system, and insisted that every rate-payer ought to have a voice in the selection of grand juries, while others such as the MP for Dublin University, Thomas Lefroy, defended grand juries and opposed any encroachment on their powers.[120] Much of the comment outside parliament focussed on the issue of representation. Liberal commentators such as the editorial writers of the *Northern Whig* welcomed the proposed alterations as likely to prevent jobbing but regretted that the principle of election had not been extended to grand juries.[121] Conservatives on the other hand interpreted the proposals as an attack on the Irish gentry and their position in the Irish countryside. A speaker at a meeting of the Conservative Society in Belfast in February 1833 was reported by the *Belfast Newsletter* to have delivered a stirring defence of the grand jury system, arguing that the present bill was an attempt to follow up the reform bill and 'still further to lessen and degrade the consequence and rank of the gentry'. If the bill was passed, he warned, assizes would be turned into a 'public debating shop, open to every ruffian that may enter and subject to the criticism and denunciation of every cottage Hampden and every local agitator'.[122]

The problem for the government was that the bill had roused the ire of the Irish gentry without satisfying the critics of the system. Comments sent to the select committee appointed to consider the bill questioned the practicality of many of the provisions and particularly that exempting tenants at will from payment of county cess which, it was felt, would merely induce landlords to increase rents and prevent leases being granted. The committee recommended that the bill be postponed but ministers were determined to press ahead, claiming that it would effect real improvements. They did, however, agree to a number of amendments, including the omission of the clauses exempting tenants from paying cess together with the reintroduction of a property qualification for magistrates at special sessions. It was further announced that the bill would not come into effect until the following year.[123] Despite continued criticism of the bill both inside and outside parliament, its passage was welcomed by a number of Irish newspapers on the grounds that any departure from the old system would be an improvement. The *Kilkenny Journal*, for example, identified three valuable principles contained in the measure, giving cess-payers a voice in and control over their own taxation, executing all work by tender and placing all public works under the superintendence of a qualified surveyor.[124]

The formation in April 1835 of a new whig government under Lord Melbourne, openly supported by O'Connell, was greeted as heralding a new era for Ireland. Although it was the character of the Irish administration, headed by Lords Mulgrave and Morpeth, and its declared policy of seeking the support and participation of the catholic population which was its most significant innovation, a number of the legislative reforms enacted in the years between 1835 and 1841 were of lasting importance. Acts reshaping the police force, the poor relief system and municipal government established structures which were to survive for the remainder of the century. Underlying these reforms was a desire to improve the quality of local administration and to make it more acceptable to the mass of the population. To this end it was necessary to loosen the stranglehold which protestant landowners exercised over local government. The fact that those whose interests were most directly threatened were the Tory opponents of the government only served to intensify the opposition to the proposed reforms. As far as grand juries were concerned, however, ministers adopted a conciliatory approach. The bill produced in 1836 to consolidate and amend the laws relating to grand juries contained no more than a nod in the direction of popular representation by increasing the number of cess-payers at road sessions. (If the cess-payers failed to attend sessions magistrates could act without them.)[125] This modest reform nevertheless provoked opposition from those who feared that cess-payers might outnumber magistrates.[126] The bill was subsequently amended to remove the property qualification for magistrates at roads sessions, thus enabling any magistrate of the county to attend and vote. At the same time, and to prevent magistrates blocking necessary repairs, cess-payers were granted the right to petition the lord lieutenant to direct work to be undertaken if repairs were neglected. County surveyors were also empowered to make applications, if none had been made, for public works they considered necessary.[127] An attempt by William Smith O'Brien to introduce an amendment which would provide for the election of parochial wardens to represent their districts at presentment sessions in association with magistrates seems to have attracted little support. Under O'Brien's plan those attending presentment sessions would elect from their number a fiscal board for the area, to which all the fiscal powers and duties of the grand jury would be transferred.[128] The reluctance of English ministers to contemplate elections in the Irish counties should cause little surprise given their opposition to local elections in England. In June 1836 the radical MP, Joseph Hume, introduced a bill to create elected county boards to take over the financial functions of magistrates in quarter sessions. A number of Irish MPs enthusiastically supported the measure and expressed the hope that the same principle would be extended to Ireland.[129] Speaking for the government, Lord John Russell conceded that it was difficult to make any objection to the principle of Hume's bill but opposed it as impractical, claiming that it would create expensive offices and thus increase county rates.[130]

The level of county rates was a contentious issue in both Ireland and England and the 1836 grand jury act was criticised for its failure to address the problem of compulsory presentments, which accounted for an increasing proportion of county expenditure. Figures quoted in a report on Irish grand jury laws prepared by a committee of the grand jury of County Down in 1831 indicate that imperative presentments made up over 25% of total assessments in 1830 compared to just under 11% in 1802.[131] A commons select committee appointed in 1836 to inquire into compulsory presentments concluded that grand juries had reason to feel aggrieved at a system which required them to authorise expenditure which they could neither examine nor control. Before the constabulary act of 1836, for example, the only document presented to the grand jury regarding the cost of constabulary force in the county was a certificate from the privy council stating the sum required. The constabulary act did at least require constabulary accounts to be submitted to the county authorities, but the grand jury had no power to query the accounts or to refuse to grant a presentment if they found them unsatisfactory. Stressing the need for an urgent reduction in compulsory presentments, the select committee recommended that central government should bear the full cost of items such as the militia establishment, and that there should be greater local control over expenditure in other areas.[132] Levels of government funding were gradually increased. To take just two examples, the full cost of the constabulary force was taken onto the consolidated fund in 1846, and in 1875 the government took over a portion of the expense of lunatic asylums, which grand juries were required to fund but whose management was entrusted to government appointed boards, providing 4s per patient per week, a yearly contribution that amounted to around two-fifths of the average cost of a patient's upkeep.[133] Ministers were also careful to avoid imposing any further responsibilites upon grand juries in matters of public health and welfare. In the future these were to fall on the shoulders not of grand jurors but of poor law guardians.

The poor law system established in 1838, and funded by a separate poor rate, had provided an alternative structure on which central government could build.[134] Administered by boards of guardians composed partly of members elected by the ratepayers and partly of local magistrates sitting ex officio, the system had the advantage of being seen to be more representative of the interests of ratepayers and of

ordinary people than other county bodies and, despite dislike of the
workhouses themselves, the boards of guardians enjoyed a level of
popular acceptability which grand juries never acquired. The direction of local dispensaries was transferred from the grand juries to the
poor law authorities in 1851, and under later health and safety legislation such as the sanitary act of 1866, and the public health acts of
1874 and 1878, it was the boards which acted as the administering
authority. The growing importance of poor law boards in county
administration is evident in expenditure levels. Union expenditure
decreased in the years after the Famine but then began to rise again,
growing from a level of around £750,000 p.a. in the mid-1850s to
almost £1.4 million in 1886.[135] Grand jury expenditure, on the other
hand, remained fairly static in the second half of the nineteenth century. Yearly returns of county cess had increased from around
£400,000 in 1803 to nearly £1.3 million in 1840. The figure for 1896–7
was £1.2 million.[136] In the late eighteenth and early nineteenth centuries new powers and responsibilities had been imposed on grand
juries as the most convenient local body. The second half of the century saw their return to their original and primary function, that of
roads authorities. By the end of the century this aspect of their work
had been extended to cover railways. Under the Tramway and Public
Companies (Ireland) Act of 1883,[137] grand juries were empowered to
raise money for the contruction of a line of railway in their district so
long as the line was in use and efficiently maintained.

Because their members were drawn from a smaller section of the
community, grand jury meetings rarely became the political battle-
grounds which those of poor law boards and urban bodies came on
occasions to resemble later in the century, but this is not to say that
they held no interest for members of the public. Standing resolutions
approved by the grand jury of County Sligo at the summer assizes of
1864 indicate that Sligo grand jurors believed that their proceedings
were arousing too much public interest. It was resolved that during
the transaction of fiscal business no person who was not a member of
the grand jury had the right to offer any observation upon a presentment, and that permission must be obtained from the foreman of the
jury before any such person could be heard. Noting that on many
recent occasions great inconvenience had been occasioned from the
admission of deputations consisting of unlimited numbers of persons,
it was resolved that deputations should not be admitted without the
assent of the majority of the jurors and should not exceed three
gentlemen.[138] Public criticism of the grand jury system, while it did not
die away altogether,[139] was more muted in the later half of the
nineteenth century than it had been in earlier decades. Grand juries
were still dominated by the landlord class and resented as such, but a

number of factors combined to make them less objectionable to the population as a whole. Legislative reforms, culminating in the grand jury act of 1836, did limit opportunities for abuse of grand jury powers and helped to improve standards of administration. More important perhaps was the fact that not only did county cess cease its relentless upward path, but that from 1870 small tenants were relieved from its burden. Under all tenancy agreements entered into after the land act of 1870, tenants were entitled to deduct half the cess owing on the land from their rent where their holding was valued at more than £4. Where the holding was worth less than £4, the entire sum could be deducted from the rent or was to be paid by the landlord. The major part of the burden of county cess was thus thrown on landlords, providing some justification for their dominant role in county management, at a time when the increasing vitality and urgency of the national question was in any case diverting attention from local grievances.

Local Government in Rural Areas
C. Poor Law Boards

A special report prepared for the select committee on local government and taxation, and published in 1878, judged the poor law union to constitute 'the most important of the several organizations into which the local government of Ireland divides itself'. The tendency of modern legislation, the report further observed, 'has steadily set in the direction of availing of the many advantages presented by union organization and machinery for the performance of various new and important functions'.[140] As originally introduced in 1838, the poor law was a limited measure intended to provide a safety net for those from the poorest class who were facing destitution. It was designed to deter all but the desperate from applying for assistance, in the belief that any more widely based system of poor relief would be both prohibitively expensive and morally debilitating. The fear of creating a culture of dependency which had influenced the framers of the 1834 poor law amendment act in England, was even more powerful in Ireland, where catholic tenants were regarded by their landlords as being naturally lazy. Limited as it was, the poor law remained the primary source of poor relief into the twentieth century. It created the basic structure upon which a social services system was gradually established, providing not only poor relief, but also medical care and health services generally. Even after its formal abolition, the poor law system continued to influence the character and administration of social services in Ireland. Home assistance given under the Irish government's public assistance act of 1939, for example, bore striking similarities to outdoor relief given under the poor law from 1847, while the dispensary service established by the medical charities act of 1851, which provided a medical service for poor people outside the workhouse, continued to operate virtually unchanged in the independent Irish state until 1970.[141]

Information on the extent of poverty in Ireland was widely available in the early years of the nineteenth century. House of commons select committees inquired into the condition of the poorer classes in 1804, 1819, 1823 and 1830 and their findings were supplemented by the accounts of journalists and travellers, who rarely failed to comment upon the sight of ragged beggars lining the roadsides, and more generally on the wretched circumstances in which so many of the Irish peasantry existed. Poverty was seen as a crucial factor in the disorder which plagued the country and many of those urging the need for reforms put great stress on the effect these would have on the disposition of the people. In his influential *Letters on the State of Ireland*, published in 1825 under the acronym J.K.L., Dr Doyle, Bishop of Kildare and Leighlin, condemned the state of law and society, and warned that there could be neither peace nor security in Ireland until the people could put their trust in government. If the laws discriminating against catholics were repealed and a poor rate introduced, 'it will produce peace and order, not by terror and compulsion, as at present, but by self-interest and attachment to the law'.[142] Such arguments appealed to British politicians who believed that economic and social conditions were the real cause of discontent in Ireland and that if these were removed the country would become loyal and peaceful. Real distress, Anglesey declared in a letter to Grey early in 1831, 'is a fearful ally to traitorous agitation'.[143] Anglesey placed much of the blame for the perpetual excitement of the people squarely upon the shoulders of Irish landowners: 'the poor, wretched people are literally starving . . . The landlord rigidly exacts his rent, or distrains for it, and the tithe-proctor mercilessly drives the cattle, with a perfect knowledge of the total inability of the owner to pay what the composition requires. If they were not the most enduring people upon earth they would not bear their hardships as they do'.[144]

By the 1830s pressure for the introduction of some form of poor relief was growing. The issue was one which cut across party and religious lines and it was partly to avoid division within their own party that whig ministers responded to a proposal in 1833 to extend the English poor law to Ireland by announcing the appointment of a royal commission to investigate the issue. The story of the Whateley commission and the rejection of its report which recommended the initiation of large-scale public works, state sponsored emigration and local provision for the care of the sick, elderly and lunatic poor, in favour of a measure modelled on the English workhouse system, is well known.[145] Russell's introduction in 1837 of a bill closely following the English poor law act of 1834 is generally interpreted as the action of a minister clutching at a convenient and simplistic solution to the problem of Irish poverty in preference to the more complex, and therefore probably more appropriate, programme of action advocated by the Whateley commission. But this, as a recent study by Peter Grey has indicated,[146] is to misunderstand the political context in which the bill was proposed and the motivation of those ministers most closely identified with it, Russell, Morpeth and Mulgrave. The Irish poor law must be considered in conjunction with other measures enacted during these years, such as reform of the tithe system and of municipal corporations, which, it was hoped, would win the hearts and minds of the catholic community by redressing outstanding grievances. Just as the appointment of catholics to positions of responsibility was intended to attach the catholic middle classes to the government, so the poor law was intended to given hope to the peasantry. In his speech introducing the poor relief bill in February 1837, Russell argued that the lack of a poor law in Ireland had produced,

> on the one hand the most extensive mendicancy, and on the other the most extensive crime. It has produced, too, a third consequence, namely, the indifference or neglect on the part of landlords as to the manner in which their property is cultivated and their tenants live.

The bill would act, he insisted, as a promoter of social concord, 'showing a disposition in the state and in the community at large to attend to the welfare of all classes' and interesting 'the landowner and persons of property in the country in the welfare of their tenants and their neighbours'.[147]

The determination that Irish property must support Irish poverty was a significant factor behind the attachment of Russell, Morpeth and others to the poor law. Indeed, the appropriate role to be played by Irish landlords in this matter was to provide a subtext to the debate on the bill in parliament. One of the things uniting the disparate forces in favour of the bill, from liberal whigs to humanist tories, was the belief that Irish landlords were failing in their responsibilities to their tenants and to society in general. The opponents of the measure on the other hand, from O'Connell to Lord Lyndhurst, believed that the bill would make matters worse by persuading both landlords and tenants to look to the state rather than their own resources. Lyndhurst made much in his attacks on the bill of the power which would reside in the centrally-appointed poor law commissioners who were to supervise the operation of the act.[148] This element of central control was typical of whig reforms of these years. Lyndhurst ignored the fact that the bill also provided for a far greater degree of control by ratepayers than any previous measure relating to local administration in rural areas. The introduction of elections for poor law guardians (elected guardians were to serve alongside local magistrates acting ex officio, in a ratio of three-quarters elected to one quarter ex officio) was a radical departure in terms of Irish county government the consequences of which were only to become fully apparent in later decades.

Important as the political background to the act is, the fact remained that to those at the receiving end of the legislation, it did not appear as a radical or generous measure. The act was deliberately framed to make the relief available as unpalatable as possible, and since it was difficult to create conditions in Irish workhouses which would actually be worse than those outside, it was hoped that a strict regime and a severely limited diet would deter all but the very poorest and most desperate from applying to enter the workhouse. Relief, which was to be granted at the discretion of the guardians (meaning that no-one, however destitute, had a statutory right to relief) was limited to relief in the workhouse. A preference was to be given to the aged, the infirm, the defective and children. After these persons had been provided for, the guardians were at liberty to relieve others, and if accommodation in the workhouse was insufficient priority was to be given to people resident in the union. (Under the act the country was divided up into unions, composed of electoral divisions made up of townlands.) Relief provided by the guardians was subject to the directions and control of the poor law commissioners, though the commissioners were prohibited from interfering in individual cases.

The Irish poor law system was established as an off-shoot from the English system. George Nicholls, who had been sent over to Ireland by Russell in 1836 to report on the feasibility of introducing the English system there, was appointed commissioner for Ireland together with four English assistant commissioners, a further four being appointed later in Ireland. The commissioners divided the country into 130 unions containing 2,049 electoral divisions, each of which returned at least one representative. They also set the value of the property qualifications by which people would be eligible to stand for the office of guardian. The act provided for different qualifications for different electoral districts to secure a genuinely popular representation. In the second half of the nineteenth century the average qualification was a rating level of around £20, with the lowest being just £6 in parts of County Mayo.[149] The poor rate was levied on both owners and occupiers of land in equal parts and both groups were granted votes. Highly rated occupiers were given multiple votes (up to a maximum of six), and men who were both owners and occupiers were able to utilise their votes in both respects. Furthermore, owners unlike occupiers could vote by proxy. The voting system was thus weighted in favour of property owners, who were in any case ensured representation on poor law boards in the persons of ex officio guardians drawn from the local magistracy. Under the original act every justice of the peace residing in a union and acting for the county in which he resided was entitled to sit as an ex officio guardian, providing that he was not a stipendiary magistrate, or in holy orders, so long as the total number of ex officio members of the board did not exceed one-third of the elected guardians or one-quarter of the total number of guardians on the board. If there were too many eligible magistrates they were to elect representatives from amongst themselves. The proportion of ex officio guardians was increased following the passage of an act in 1843 which exempted occupiers of property rated at less than £4 p.a. from the poor rate, and made their portion of the rates chargeable to the owner. Landowners were thus made responsible for over 60% of poor rates in Ireland. As compensation, the proportion of ex officio guardians permitted to serve on any board was increased from one-third to one-half.[150]

The machinery of the poor law was installed relatively quickly. By 1842, 122 workhouses were ready with accommodation for around 100,000 inmates, although in the years before the Famine the numbers being relieved at any one time rarely exceeded 40,000.[151] The introduction of the poor rate did meet opposition in some areas, mainly in the west. A parliamentary return covering the period from January 1843 to January 1844 listed twenty-one unions as requiring police or military assistance to enforce the collection of rates,[152] and it was partly to prevent such scenes in the future that the lowest rated properties were exempted from the poor rate in 1843. In their annual report published in 1846, the poor law commissioners expressed satisfaction with the progress of the poor law in Ireland. All the workhouses originally proposed were then open, and rates were being collected in the vast majority of unions.[153] In executing their functions, the poor law commissioners were influenced by a strong belief in the wide-ranging benefits which the new system would confer upon Ireland. As R.B. McDowell has noted, they considered themselves

> not merely departmental officials engaged in guaranteeing the indigent Irish man from starvation, but warriors in a great administrative crusade. The poor law system, they were convinced, was bound to play a mighty part in inaugurating a new era in public life, when the prevalence of official impartiality, efficiency, economy and standardised and scientific methods of administration would raise the moral tone of the whole community. In the meantime the respectable as guardians, and the poor as paupers, were to be taught by experience the practical expression of the most recent and soundest political theory.[154]

The tone adopted by the commissioners in their communications with boards, and their interference in even the smallest details of workhouse administration, understandably irritated many guardians. In a debate in the commons in 1842, O'Connell claimed that the commissioners had increased their unpopularity

> by the flippancy and impertinence of their expressions; and the determination too, that they would not yield to local feelings and circumstances but maintain their own "cast iron" system.

There was a widespread impression, O'Connell continued, that the commissioners were motivated by 'political partialities and religious prejudices'.[155]

The experience of the Famine was crucial to the development of the Irish poor law.[156] Not only did the poor law itself undergo amendment to extend its scope, but the perceived failure of Irish landowners to organise relief schemes contributed to the increasingly marginal role assigned to them in matters of local administration in the second half of the nineteenth century. The workhouse system had never been intended, and was not designed, to cope with the results of widespread famine and the government's initial response to the failure of the potato crop was to introduce temporary relief measures separate from the poor law and relying on local initiative. This approach, which reflected the concern of Peel and his ministers to support but not supersede local efforts, was continued under the whig government headed by Russell which took office in 1846. By the end of 1846, however, it was clear that the public works programme was insufficient to deal with the magnitude of the crisis. The number of starving and destitute people was increasing and with workhouses full to overflowing many unions were already providing some form of outdoor relief, despite being forbidden to do so under the act of 1838.[157]

In January 1847 the government announced its intention to end public works as a means of relief and to administer aid directly. An act providing for direct distribution of food was passed in February 1847 as a temporary measure until a reformed workhouse system could take over as the main provider of relief. Permanent change was effected by the poor law extension act[158] which was approved by parliament later that summer. The act created a separate poor law commission for Ireland with powers to alter existing union boundaries[159] and to appoint inspectors to supervise the administration of unions. In a major departure from the provisions of the original poor law act of 1838, the right to relief of certain groups (those classed as destitute who were disabled by reason of age, infirmity or mental deficiency, together with destitute widows having two or more legitimate children dependent upon them) was recognised and out-door relief sanctioned in periods of 'unusual distress', though this could only be provided for the able-bodied poor if the workhouse was full. Under an amendment to the act, anyone occupying more than a quarter of an acre of land was excluded from receiving relief. The effect of this clause, combined with landlords' liability for poor rates on holdings worth less than £4 p.a. and falling rent rolls, was to encourage landlords to evict their smallest tenants who were forced into already over-crowded workhouses. A total of 417,139 people were relieved in workhouses in 1847. By the end of 1849 this figure had risen to 932,284.[160]

The establishment of an independent poor law commission in Ireland enabled the government to place the full burden of financial responsibility for poor relief on the Irish taxpayer. In the areas worst affected by the Famine, the burden proved too heavy. Poor law boards in the south and west found it impossible either to collect rates or to pay back loans already taken out. Under the poor law extension act, the commissioners had the power to dissolve boards whose members were incompetent or neglected their duties. This step was taken with reluctance as the commissioners were anxious not to encourage guardians to evade their responsibilities however irksome or unpleasant, but between August 1847 and March 1849 thirty-nine boards of guardians were suspended and paid officials appointed to take their place.[161] Faced with the complete collapse of the agricultural infrastructure in parts of the country, the Irish commissioners declared twenty-three unions (all, except one union in Donegal, in the provinces of Munster and Connaught) to be 'distressed' and thus in need of external aid, but their requests for more money to be made available from the imperial exchequer met strong opposition in Britain. The government did agree to advance a further £100,000 to be repaid by a levy of 6d in the £ in the more prosperous unions, with an additional grant of £50,000 for the immediate use of 'distressed' unions.[162] By acknowledging that individual unions could no longer be expected to support their own poor, the rate-in-aid scheme represented a departure from a fundamental principle of the poor law system, that poor relief should be a local charge. The change, which made poor relief a national but not an imperial charge, was fiercely resented by unions, particularly those in Ulster, on which the additional levy was made. Ratepayers in these unions objected to being asked to subsidise what they saw as the results of incompetence elsewhere. In some parts of Ulster resistance to the collection of the rate-in-aid resulted in significant arrears. At the end of 1851, Cookstown in County Tyrone had collected only 5% of the amount due. This was exceptional, however, and the action of a few unions failed to halt the imposition of the levy.[163] Total expenditure under the poor law exceeded £2 million in 1849, much of this being spent on the provision of additional workhouse accommodation. In July of that year there were over one million people receiving relief, of whom 221,583 were in workhouses and 784,367 receiving outdoor relief.[164] Due to the good harvest, the situation did ease somewhat during 1849, though mortalities remained high, and by November all but five of the dissolved boards had been reinstated.[165]

Whatever its failings as a means of preventing deaths by starvation and disease, the Irish poor law system had demonstrated its capacity to provide relief with reasonable efficiency to large numbers of destitute people. The relatively prosperous decades which followed the Famine were to see the expansion of the responsibilities of boards of guardians to encompass a wide range of specialised welfare services. Perhaps the most important development in this respect was the passage of the medical charities act in 1851, which created a national machinery for supplying medical services and brought a medical practitioner into every district. Previously people had only been able to obtain medical help in workhouse hospitals, in county infirmaries, and as out-patients at voluntary dispensaries established under the act of 1805.[166] Such dispensaries were badly equipped and their distribution across the country was patchy. For the vast majority of people there was no home medical relief available, since dispensary doctors only visited patients who lived within a short distance of the dispensary. Under the act of 1851 the country was divided into dispensary districts each with a qualified medical officer whose services were to be paid for out of the poor rate. (From 1867 the government paid half the salary of the dispensary doctor and met the costs of a midwife, if appointed, and of medicines dispensed.) The dispensary service was administered by committees composed partly of poor law guardians and partly of ratepayers chosen by the guardians on a yearly basis. In 1878 there were 720 such committees supervising the operation of 1,088 dispensary stations and a staff of 804 medical officers, 41 compounders (pharmacists) and 217 midwives. The number of people who received medical relief under this system was impressive. During the year to September 1876, the total number afforded relief was 670,750, of whom 481,331 were seen at dispensaries and 189,419 at home. The cost of the service for that year was £141,463, roughly 13% of total poor law expenditure.[167] Until 1862 workhouse hospitals were restricted to treating the destitute sick, but the poor law amendment act of that year opened these institutions to the sick generally. The same act provided for the boarding out of orphans and deserted children and repealed the so-called Gregory clause which had prevented those with holdings of more than a quarter of an acre from claiming relief.[168]

As central government assumed increasing responsibility for public health, so the powers and duties of poor law boards expanded. The nuisance removal acts of 1848, 1855 and 1860, for example, empowered boards of guardians to appoint sanitary committees from among their number and to cause any property deemed to to be a health hazard to be removed at the owner's expense. If the owner could not afford to do this, the guardians could pay for the removal out of the rates.[169] From 1856 boards of guardians acted as burial boards, and from 1865 as sewer authorities, for those portions of counties which did not fall within the jurisdiction of town authorities. The following year the sanitary act provided for the appointment of sanitary committees consisting either entirely of guardians or partly of guardians and partly of ratepayers, with powers to erect sewers and to prevent water supplies being contaminated by sewage. The act also created a new post of sanitary inspector, to be paid from the rates, to service the committees and advise on matters such as drainage and the supply of clean water. Guardians' responsibilities were further increased by the public health acts of 1874 and 1878 which made the poor law boards rural sanitary authorities, increased the number of sanitary staff and gave them new powers to destroy unsound food, supervise slaughter houses and deal with infectious diseases in hospitals.[170] Poor law boards were sometimes slow to exercise their powers under these acts, being reluctant to sanction the necessary increase in local taxation. Responding to a letter from Joseph Eaton of Belfast drawing attention to the state of Maghera Cross burial ground in September 1876, the clerk of the Irvinestown board of guardians explained that the board had already taken the matter into consideration 'but decline to tax the union with the cost of repairing the same, as they considered it should be repaired by private subscription'.[171] Some years earlier, a circular from the poor law commission had rebuked boards of guardians who had discontinued their employment of sanitary inspectors on the grounds that their district was free of cholera. The powers of the sanitary act were not directed against cholera alone, the circular reminded guardians, and matters such as the removal of nuisances, the maintenance of proper drainage, the supply of pure water and the prevention of over-crowding were 'objects which the legislature has determined shall henceforth be continuously carried out for the security of public health and has therefore created permanent powers and imposed permanent responsibilities'. In the discharge of their duties, the circular concluded, guardians must be prepared to incur some additional expenditure, but since this would act as a preventative to disease it would actually save money in the future.[172]

Other acts which imposed duties on poor law boards included the marriage registration act of 1844, the vagrant act of 1847, the parliamentary voters act of 1850 the common lodging-houses acts of 1851, 1853 and 1860, the bake-house registration act of 1863, the cattle diseases acts of 1866, 1870 and 1876, the workshops regulation act of 1867 and the rivers pollution act of 1877.[173] Towards the end of the century boards also became involved in the improvement of rural housing under the provisions of the labourers acts. Six acts were passed between 1883 and 1896 enabling guardians to undertake improvement schemes in districts where the existing accommodation for agricultural labourers was inadequate. Boards of guardians could borrow money from the commissioners of public works to build new houses, complete with garden allotments, which were then let to labourers. All schemes had to be approved by the local government board.[174] Up to the end of 1896 the local government board sanctioned the building of 14,831 cottages, financed by treasury loans of £1.75 million.[175] Generally speaking it was only guardians in Leinster and Munster who made use of this legislation. In November 1885, the board of guardians of Irvinestown in County Fermanagh recorded their opinion that there was no necessity to build any labourers' houses at present, although they instructed sanitary sub-officers to make a 'minute inspection' of all such houses in the union to see that they were in a fit state.[176] Promotion of improvement schemes, together with the growing number of officials employed by the guardians in various capacities, helped to push up poor law expenditure from around £0.5 million in 1859 to over £1 million in 1876 and around £1.5 million in 1895.[177] Membership of a poor law board provided access to an important decision-making process as well as to a significant source of patronage. Poor law boards were no longer involved simply in the distribution of relief. They had become an increasingly important branch of local government. Their role in local administration was given statutory recognition in 1872[178] when the poor law commission was abolished and the supervisory role of the commissioners was transferred to the newly-constituted local government board for Ireland.

In the early years of the poor law system landowners managed to impose a large measure of control on boards of guardians both by serving as ex officio guardians, and by exerting their influence over elections to ensure that compliant tenants, or in many cases their own agents, were elected. The presence of the latter was particularly important since many landowners were absentees, while those who were active in their locality were also in demand as magistrates, sheriffs and grand jurors. The voting system in poor law elections was weighted in favour of landowners by means of cumulative voting, but tenants, who far outnumbered landowners, could outvote their landlords so long as they voted together. Too heavy-handed an intervention in poor law elections could, however, be counter-productive. The year after the passage of the poor law act in 1838, the Reverend F. Blakely of Crossnacreevy in County Down wrote to Lord Downshire's agent at Hillsborough, W.E. Reilly, to warn him that a feeling hostile to Downshire's interest was being created by persons going around delivering verbal messages as if from Downshire and Reilly himself, concerning the forthcoming election in the Moneyrea electoral division of the Newtownards poor law union. Any interference would, Blakely suggested, be particularly imprudent since the candidates nominated at a recent meeting of cess-payers were in fact favourable to Downshire. Recommending that Reilly should be neutral about the guardianship, Blakely commented that Lord

Londonderry had one townland in the same division, 'but he has wisely kept neutral'.[179]

An analysis of the elections for poor law guardians held in 1839 and 1840 by Gerard O'Brien has indicated the extent to which the contests were fought along party lines, with many elections being reduced to power-struggles between local priests and landlords.[180] Political issues, both local and national, remained a crucial factor in the elections to, and functioning of, poor law boards. Reporting on the state of County Wexford in March 1848, Lord Carew warned the viceroy, Lord Clarendon, that

> the repeal agitators for their private interests, and the patronage, have taken possession of the Corporation, poor law boards, etc. This last has made the wish among the proprietors to have paid, impartial, responsible guardians, at least for the present.[181]

The boards were the only administrative body in rural areas with directly elected representatives and as such provided a rare platform from which individuals from the catholic middle classes could acquire local prominence and influence. In the later decades of the century membership of a board acted as a stepping-stone to other positions. Many of those who entered public life as elected poor law guardians went on to serve as county councillors, and some as members of parliament. At least seven members of Parnell's parliamentary party, following the election of 1885, had come up through the ranks of poor law guardians.[182] During the land war poor law boards were specifically targeted by the land league as potential power bases from which to carry on the fight against landlord power. In 1873 *The Nation* had published an editorial urging that poor law elections should be fought on the home rule issue,[183] but it was not until the 1880s that this was taken up on anything like a nationwide basis. In a comprehensive study of poor law elections between 1872 and 1886, W.L. Feingold concluded that the political balance on poor law boards was significantly altered in the years following Parnell's appeal to the Irish people on 1 March 1881, through the pages of the *Freeman's Journal*, to seize control of every board of guardians in the country. Using the percentage of board officers drawn from the landlord class as an indication of the extent to which the boards were subject to landlord influence, Feingold found that this percentage dropped from 88% in 1877 to 51% in 1886, representing what he interpreted as a transfer of power from landlords to tenants.[184] This analysis inevitably over-simplifies a complex process – the categorisation of office-holders being a crude definition of political allegiance – but it does highlight the role of local institutions in furthering political developments which are too often discussed only in a national context. The fusion of national and local issues is particularly evident in the involvement of land league branches in poor law elections. Feingold emphasised that whereas Parnell and other national leaders showed little interest in the activities of poor law guardians, local branches of the land league continued to involve themselves in elections and in board proceedings.[185] Many activists were quick to see the opportunities provided by the boards, as by the league itself, to establish themselves as local figures. A good example of this is provided by the career of John Heffernan, a businessman from Kildare town, who helped to found a land league branch in the town in 1880. Heffernan features in Thomas Nelson's study of local politics in County Kildare during the land war, in which he describes how Heffernan was an unsuccessful candidate in the election for the poor law board of the Naas union in 1881, finally gaining a place the following year. In November 1882 he became secretary of the Kildare town branch of the national league. Through his work for the league, Heffernan was able to build up a network of local contacts which were to ease his passage into county council politics. In 1899 he served as chairman of the Naas No. 1 rural district council and became secretary of the Kildare county council the following year.[186]

The increasingly politicised character of poor law boards was evident in their activities. Nationalist dominated boards were anxious to use their powers to aid tenant farmers, through the granting of outdoor relief to evicted tenants, for example, or by building cottages for agricultural labourers. Speaking in the house of lords in 1898, the Marquess of Londonderry referred to the 'prostitution of outdoor relief' that had taken place in unions which had returned nationalist members after 1881. Not only had the amount expended dramatically increased (he quoted the example of the Listowel union where the numbers receiving outdoor relief had risen from 258 people in 1880 at a total cost of £65 per week, to 2,187 people in 1884 at a cost of £1,638 per week), but relief was being granted to people who did not qualify for it. Families, he claimed, had been granted £1 a week even though they were in possession of horses, sheep and cattle. He recalled that as viceroy in 1886 he had been forced to dissolve the board of the union of New Ross after the guardians had relaxed workhouse rules in favour of evicted tenants, despite warnings that their proceedings were irregular.[187] The actions of some nationalist guardians brought them into conflict with the law. In March 1890 Timothy Clarke, a poor law guardian for Looscam in the Portumna union in County Galway, was sentenced by magistrates in Loughrea to three months imprisonment in default of paying the sum of £47 which was a surcharge imposed by the auditor in respect of money given on Clarke's authority as relief to evicted tenants. Clarke refused to pay the surcharge, presenting his refusal as a political matter, and was imprisoned in Galway gaol. Reporting these facts to the Castle, the local police sergeant hinted at another reason for Clarke's reluctance to pay. More than the amount of the surcharge had apparently been collected from sympathisers, 'which he can have for himself when he is out of gaol'.[188] Political divisions could have a paralysing effect on board discussions. A member of the Clogher board of guardians in County Tyrone apologised to a fellow guardian for his absence from a meeting in 1893, commenting 'I hope to God the Home Rulers did not get the better of you today. They should not get anything that we could keep from them right or wrong'.[189]

Concluding his study of poor law boards in the 1870s and 80s, Feingold argued that the boards gave tenant farmers experience of the political process within the political system on a regular basis, providing an important preparation for self-government.[190] They provided an equally important training ground for women, who became eligible to serve as poor law guardians in 1896 and whose labours as guardians would, it was believed, demonstrate their fitness for other civic responsibilities, including that of voting in parliamentary elections. Women were felt to have certain qualities which would be particularly valuable to the boards, namely their capacity for selfless devotion to others and their knowledge of matters such as dietary requirements, health and childcare. Supporting a bill introduced in 1896 by the Belfast MP, William Johnston, to enable women to act as guardians, the Marquess of Londonderry observed that

> there was a strong feeling in Ireland, especially in Ulster, that there was a certain sphere of work in which the services of woman on boards of guardians would be of great value. Thus they could look after pauper women and children, the training of girls for service, and the food and sanitary arrangements far better than men.[191]

Despite opposition in parliament from those who believed that being a poor law guardian was not a suitable occupation for a woman, and from nationalist MPs who argued that any reform should address the mode of election of guardians generally,[192] the bill received the blessing of the government on the grounds that it brought the situation in Ireland into line with that in England, and it passed into law that summer. The first two women to serve as guardians were elected at by-elections in Lisbellaw in County Fermanagh and Limavady in County Londonderry, shortly after the passage of the act. The following year saw thirteen women elected in unions from Fermanagh to Kerry and by 1898 there were twenty-two women guardians.[193] Women rarely stood on any political platform in poor law elections and voters may have found their candidacy attractive on that account, feeling that

they would address themselves to the job in hand. Anna Haslam
noted that

> in one of our Dublin elections [in 1898] there is good reason to believe
> that not only did several hundred women vote for the lady candidate, but
> in a large number of cases they rose above sectarian prejudices, and gave
> her their votes, though she belongs to a different church to themselves,
> simply because she is well known for her deeds of mercy to the poor, and
> can be absolutely trusted to do her duty by them.[194]

Women did well in the poor law elections for 1899 (the first to be held
under the local government act of 1898). Eighty-five were elected,
many to unions in which there were already women guardians,
although a report on the elections by Haslam conceded that 'owing to
the elections having been run very much upon party lines, several
ladies who have been doing most excellent work in their respective
unions during the past year – more particularly in Belfast and Co.
Dublin – have not been re-elected, and the loss from this cause is very
deplorable'.[195] The impact of women was already being felt on poor
law administration. According to Haslam, the influence of women
had been productive of valuable reforms in the two Dublin workhouses and in the unions of Belfast, Derry and Coleraine, 'and the
same is true of the Rathdown Union, where a large proportion of the
children have been boarded-out during the past year'.[196]

The full effect of the entry of women to poor law boardrooms has
yet to be analysed. Some idea of the problems facing reform-minded
guardians, whether women or men, can be gained from Susanne R.
Day's satirical novel, *The Amazing Philanthropists*, published in
1916.[197] Day paints a vivid portrait of poor law administration, based
on her own experiences on the Cork board of guardians to which she
was elected in 1911, aged twenty-one. The novel describes the efforts
of two women guardians to improve the conditions and administration of the Ballybawn workhouse and workhouse hospital, and the
obstacles put in their way by some of their male colleagues who were
more concerned to pursue political arguments or to safeguard the
jobs of their friends and relations. 'The fence of reform', Day's central
character observes,

> is one at which the guardians refuse every time they are put at it. We are
> beginning to realise that the only way to get them over is to heave them
> over by tail or mane, neck or crop, or by any portions of their persons and
> clothing which offer grip and hoisting power ! If we waited for them to
> jump . . . [198]

Day's book was not well received. 'It was considered', we are told by
Stephen Brown and Desmond Clarke in their survey of *Ireland in Fiction*, 'an ill-natured and snobbish attack on people who are doing their
best',[199] but it remains required reading for anyone interested in the
ordinary work of a poor law guardian.

Notes

1 *Fifteenth report of the commissioners appointed to inquire into the duties, salaries and emoluments of the officers, clerks and ministers of justice in all temporal and ecclesiastical courts in Ireland: the office of sheriff*, H.C. 1826 (310), xvii, 4.
2 Fitzgerald to Finucane, 5 Sept. 1814 (N.L.I., Fitzgerld papers, MS 7834, f. 310).
3 Fitzgerald to Peel, Dec. 1814 (N.L.I., Fitzgerald papers, MS 7815, f. 224).
4 *Hansard 1*, xxxvi, 566 (14 May 1817).
5 Clendining to Sligo, 12 Sept. 1826 (N.L.I., Browne papers, MS 6403, f. 108).
6 H. Brabazon to Foster, 28 Dec. 1808 (P.R.O.N.I., Foster/Masserene papers, D562/12560).
7 Foster to W. Brabazon, 29 Jan. 1810 (ibid., D562/12638).
8 W. Brabazon to Foster, 3 Feb. 1810 (ibid., D562/12640).
9 H. Brabazon to Foster, 3 Mar. 1810 (ibid., D562/12643).
10 Stodart to Gosset, 26 Nov. 1831, Barrington to Gosset, 16 Dec. 1831 (S.P.O., Registered papers, 1831/3470).
11 *Fifteenth report of the commissioners appointed to inquire into the duties, salaries and emoluments of the officers, clerks and ministers of justice in all temporal and ecclesiastical courts in Ireland: the office of sheriff*, H.C. 1826 (310), xvii, 1–2.
12 Ibid., 12.
13 Ibid., 213.
14 Ibid., 92–94.
15 Rice to Lamb, 2 Jan. 1828 (N.L.I., Monteagle papers, MS 605/ D and E).
16 Lamb to Rice, 7 Jan. 1828 (N.L.I., Monteagle papers, MS 13368/11).
17 5 & 6 Will. IV c.55.
18 *Fifteenth report of the commissioners appointed to inquire into the duties, salaries and emoluments of the officers, clerks and ministers of justice in all temporal and ecclesiastical courts in Ireland: the office of sheriff*, H.C. 1826 (310), xvii, 22.
19 O'Connell to Mulgrave, 4 Dec. 1835 (*The Correspondence of Daniel O'Connell*, ed. M.R. O'Connell (Dublin, 1972–80), v, 2294).
20 Russell to Mulgrave, 9 Dec. 1835 (P.R.O., Russell papers, 30/22/1E, f. 258).
21 *Hansard 3*, xxxiii, 955–968 (17 May 1836).
22 Joy to Drummond, 17 May 1837; Drummond to Joy, 20 May 1837 (S.P.O., Registered papers, 1837/1456).
23 *Special report by W.P. O'Brien to the lord lieutenant upon the local government and taxation of Ireland, made in pursuance of the report of the select committee of the house of commons dated 20th July 1877*, [C 1965], H.C. 1878, xxiii, 735.
24 Jacob to Gower, 24 Aug. 1829 (S.P.O., Registered papers, 1829/8045).
25 Jacob to Gower, 7 Sept. 1829 (ibid.).
26 Gildea to Gosset, 12 Jan. 1835 (*Correspondence relative to the late elections in Ireland*, H.C. 1835 (170), xlv, 397).
27 K.T. Hoppen, *Elections, Politics and Society in Ireland 1832–1885* (Oxford, 1984), p. 417.
28 Burke to Larcom, 20 Jan. 1872; Larcom to Burke, 22 Jan. 1872 (N.L.I., Larcom papers, MS 7597).
29 *Limerick Chronicle*, 7 Aug. 1847.
30 *Report from the select committee on parliamentary and municipal elections.* H.C. 1868–9 (352), viii, 286.
31 Hackett to Burke, 19 Mar. 1880 (S.P.O., Registered papers, 1880/13150). Steel to Forster, 10 Jan. 1882 (N.L.I., Kilmainham papers, MS 1073, p. 165). This apparently prompted a strong remonstrance from the subsheriff of Cork who insisted on his legal right to requisition troops, pointing out that secrecy was vital in making seizures and that allowing even government officials to know his exact movements

would jeopardize the success of such operations. It was, a Castle official noted, 'impossible entirely to overlook the ideas of an energetic sub-sheriff who was anxious to carry out his duty in the most satisfactory manner' and it was eventually agreed to use the established procedure except when seizures were to be made when the sub-sheriff would inform the general officer at Cork directly, in communication with the county inspector. R.A.J. Hawkins, 'An Army on Police Work, 1881–2: Ross of Blandensburg's memorandum, dated 11 Dec. 1882', *Irish Sword*, xi (1973), 89.

32 40 & 41 Vict. c.56. Under this act the offices of the clerk of the peace and clerk of the crown were amalgamated and the lord lieutenant empowered to appoint a clerk of the crown and peace for each county as vacancies arose. R.B. McDowell, *The Irish Administration 1801–1914* (London, 1964), pp 132–133.

33 Caledon to Gower, 6 Oct. 1828 (P.R.O.N.I., Caledon papers, D2431/5/9A); note by Greene, Dec. 1828 (S.P.O., Registered papers, 1828/1542).

34 Abercorn to Richmond, 24 Dec. 1812 (P.R.O.N.I., Abercorn papers, D623/A/85/51), Peel to Wellesley, 12 Apr. 1822 (B.L., Peel papers, Add. MS 40324, f. 35).

35 Grey to Anglesey, 29 Dec. 1830 (P.R.O.N.I., Anglesey papers, D619/28B, f. 20).

36 Anglesey to Melbourne, 2 Jan. 1831 (ibid., D619/29B, f. 25).

37 Anglesey to Grey, 1 Jan. 1831 (ibid., D619/28C, f. 25).

38 Reprinted in the *Enniskillen Chronicle*, 27 Oct. 1831. For a list of lords lieutenant of counties from 1831 to 1850, see Appendix I.

39 *Hansard 3*, vi, 23 (15 July 1831).

40 Downshire to Anglesey, 12 Jan. 1832 (P.R.O.N.I., Anglesey papers, D619/32A/6/31), Anglesey to Downshire, 14 Jan. 1832 (ibid., D619/32G, f. 157).

41 Morpeth to Plunket, 11 Aug. 1835 (Castle Howard, Morpeth papers, J19-11-2, p. 90, by kind permission of the Howard family).

42 Morpeth to Westenra 1 Sept. 1835 (ibid., J19-11-2, p. 96).

43 *Freeman's Journal*, 16 Sept. 1869.

44 Stanley to lords lieutenant, 16 Sept. 1831 (P.R.O.N.I., Erne papers, D1939/21/9/32).

45 Circular on the duties of deputy lieutenants, Apr. 1832 (P.R.O.N.I., Downshire papers, D671/C/12/465).

46 Stanley to Gosset, 4 June 1832 (Liverpool Record Office, Derby papers, 920 DER (14) 169, f. 60).

47 Caledon to D'Arcy, 23 Sept. 1831 (P.R.O.N.I., Caledon papers, D2433/C/12/1, p. 1).

48 Caledon to clerk of peace, 23 Sept. 1831 (ibid., p. 4).

49 Caledon to Morpeth, 11 Dec. 1835 (P.R.O.N.I., Caledon papers, D2433/C/12/2, p. 53).

50 Caledon to Morpeth, 6 Oct. 1835 (ibid., p. 17).

51 Caledon to Morpeth, 11 Aug. 1836 (ibid., p. 106).

52 Petition from James Pogue and correspondence, July–Aug. 1833 (S.P.O., Registered papers, 1833/3450). See also the case of Thomas Cull, investigated by Lord Leitrim, Mar.–July 1834 (S.P.O., Reg. Paper, 1834/2737).

53 Caledon to Sinclair, 19, 26 Sept. 1838 (P.R.O.N.I., Caledon papers, D2433/C/12/2, p. 200, 202).

54 Hicks Beach to Abercorn, May 1876 (P.R.O.N.I., Abercorn papers, D623/A/317/1/16).

55 Hicks Beach to Abercorn, 15 Sept. 1876 (ibid., D623/A/318/6).

56 Carew to Forster, 26 November 1880 (S.P.O., Registered papers, 1880/29569).

57 Herdman to Belmore, 8 Aug. 1895 (P.R.O.N.I., Belmore papers, D3007/Q/1/395).

58 Herdman to Belmore, 11 Aug. 1895 (ibid., D3007/Q/1/397).

59 Number of magistrates by county including the number of roman catholics, Jan. 1834 (Staffs. Co. Record Office, Hatherton papers, D260/M/01/2058), Samuel Clark, *Social Origins of the Irish Land War* (Princeton, 1979), p. 183.

60 Memorial to Dufferin, Oct. 1869 (P.R.O.N.I., Dufferin papers, D1071H/D2/6/269).
61 Petition to Belmore, 3 Mar. 1892 (P.R.O.N.I., Belmore papers, D3007/Q/1/64).
62 *Names of all stipendiary magistrates in Ireland with the dates of their appointment and the counties in which they have served . . .* , H.C. 1831–2 (360), xxxiii, 561; K.T. Hoppen, *Elections, Politics and Society in Ireland*, p. 406.
63 *Report by the lords' select committee appointed to inquire into the state of Ireland since the year 1835, in respect of crime and outrage*, H.C. 1839 (486), xii, Q.12370.
64 Memo. on Peel's letter of 20 May 1862 (N.L.I., Larcom papers, MS 7618).
65 A useful introduction is P.J. Meghen's article, 'The Administrative Work of the Grand Jury', in *Administration*, 6, no. 3 (1958–59), 247–264. There were forty grand juries in all, one for each county and a further eight in the urban counties of Dublin, Cork, Waterford, Limerick, Kilkenny, Galway, Drogheda and Carrickfergus. In 1838 one additional grand jury was created when County Tipperary was divided into two ridings for administrative purposes, each riding having its own grand jury.
66 D. Nolan, 'The Cork Grand Jury 1836–1899', M.A. thesis (U.C.C., 1974), p. 5.
67 *Report of the royal commission on the poor laws and relief of distress: report on Ireland*, [C 4630], H.C. 1909, xxxviii, 4–5.
68 45 Geo. III c.111 (1805).
69 R.B. McDowell, 'Ireland on the eve of the Famine', in R.D. Edwards and T.D. Williams, *The Great Famine: Studies in Irish History 1845–52* (Dublin, 1956), p. 31.
70 *Special report by W.P. O'Brien to the lord lieutenant upon the local government and taxation of Ireland, made in pursuance of the report of the select committee of the house of commons dated 20th July 1877*, [C 1965], H.C. 1878, xxiii, 762–764.
71 *Report of the select committee appointed to inquire into the duties, salaries and fees of officers paid by counties in Ireland, and into the presentments compulsory upon grand juries there and to report their opinion thereon . . .* , H.C. 1836 (527), xii, 7.
72 Edward Wakefield, *An Account of Ireland, Statistical and Political* (London, 1812) p. 347.
73 Notes and Resolutions of the County Tyrone Grand Jury, 23 Mar. 1807, (P.R.O.N.I., Grand jury records, TYR/4/2/1), Hamilton to Abercorn, 28 Mar. 1807 (P.R.O.N.I., Abercorn papers, D623/A/98/14).
74 Notes and Resolutions of the County Tyrone Grand Jury, Lent 1814 (P.R.O.N.I., Grand jury records, TYR/4/2/2).
75 Barrington to Gosset, 18 Mar. 1831 (P.R.O., HO 100/237, f. 312).
76 Letters to John Foster concerning Dundalk court house, Apr.–Sept. 1812 (P.R.O.N.I., Foster papers, T2519/4/1299, /1387, /1390, /1397).
77 53 Geo. III c.131.
78 H. O'Sullivan, 'The Court House, Dundalk and the Contract for its Erection Dated 30th April, 1813, *County Louth Archeological Journal*, xv, no. 2 (1962), 131–143; Anne Crookshank, 'The Visual Arts, 1740–1850', in T.W. Moody and W.E. Vaughan (eds), *Eighteenth-Century Ireland 1691–1800* (Oxford, 1986), p. 530.
79 Hamilton to Abercorn, 11 Aug. 1804 (P.R.O.N.I., Abercorn papers, D623/A/96/26).
80 *Report from the select committee on grand jury presentments of Ireland*, H.C. 1814–15 (283), vi, 1717.
81 Knox to Sligo, 25 Mar. 1832 (N.L.I., Browne papers, MS 6403, f. 93).
82 D. Nolan, 'The Cork Grand Jury 1836–1899', M.A. Thesis (U.C.G., 1974), p. 54.
83 *Report from the select committee on grand jury presentments, Ireland*, H.C. 1826–7 (555), iii, 748–9.
84 Hutchins to Peel, 14 Feb. 1818 (B.L., Peel papers, Add. MS 40274, f. 67).
85 Jephson to Peel, 5 Sept. 1814 (B.L., Peel Papers, Add. MS 40328, f. 215).
86 'Irish Grand Juries: Mr Stanley's Bill', *The Metropolitan*, iv, no. 14 (June 1832), 145.

87 *Hansard 3*, xv, 970 (19 Feb. 1833).
88 Hamilton to Abercorn, 11 Feb. 1807 (P.R.O.N.I., Abercorn papers, D623/A/98/7).
89 Burgoyne to Abercorn, 23 Aug. 1810 (ibid., D623/A/124/36.) In 1819 agents to estates worth at least £6,000 p. a., who were also magistrates, were given the right to sit on special roads sessions summoned to investigate presentments prior to the assizes.
90 Thomas Rice, *An Inquiry into the Effect of the Irish Grand Jury Laws, as affecting the Industry, the Improvement, and the Moral Character of the People of England'* (2nd ed., London, 1815), p. 27.
91 Lambert   to   Anglesey,   11   June   1832   (P.R.O.N.I.,   Anglesey   papers, D619/32A/6/262).
92 Maria Edgeworth, *The Absentee* (1812, paperback edn. Oxford, 1988), pp 139, 142.
93 William Carleton, *Valentine M'Clutchy: the Irish Agent; or, chronicles of the Castle Cumber property* (Dublin, 1845), iii, pp 31, 57–58.
94 Orr to Fitzgerald, 18 Aug. 1809 (N.L.I., Fitzgerald papers, MS 7825).
95 County Antrim Grand Jury Resolutions and Papers, 1802–1808 (P.R.O.N.I., Grand jury records, ANT/4/7/1).
96 J.L. Foster to Foster, 5 May 1817 (P.R.O.N.I., Foster/Masserene papers, D207/74/26).
97 *Report from the select committee on grand jury presentments . . .* , H.C. 1814–15 (283), vi, 1718–19.
98 Ibid., 1731.
99 Paper by Cooper on grand jury reform, May 1817 (B.L., Peel papers, Add. MS 40265, f. 263).
100 Fitzgerald to Quin, 18 Jan. 1814 (N.L.I., Fitzgerald papers, MS 7825, f. 5).
101 *Hansard 1*, xxxvi, 959 (13 June 1817). A Bill to regulate the presenting, levying and applying of money, required for the making and repairing of public roads and buildings, and for other public purposes, under the direction of grand juries in Ireland, H.C. 1817, Public Bills ii, 357.
102 *Hansard 1*, xxxvi, 960 (13 June 1817).
103 57 Geo. III c.107.
104 Burgoyne   to   Abercorn,   16   Sept.   1817   (P.R.O.N.I.,   Abercorn   papers, D623/A/130/12/46);   Burgoyne   to   Abercorn,   31   July   1817   (ibid., D623/A/130/12/39).
105 Foster to Fitzgerald, 5 Jan. 1818 (ibid, Add MS 40210, f. 255).
106 Fitzgerald to Peel, 9 Jan. 1818 (ibid., f. 247); *Hansard 1*, xxxviii, 535 (6 May 1818).
107 58 Geo. III c.67.
108 *Dublin Evening Post*, 28 May 1818.
109 *Report form the committee on grand jury presentments in Ireland*, H.C. 1819 (378), viii, 361; *Report from the select committee on grand jury presentments, Ireland*, H.C. 1822 (353), vii, 1; *Report from the select committee on grand jury presentments, Ireland*, H.C. 1826–7 (555), iii, 745; 4 Geo. IV c.43; 7 Geo. IV c.62
110 Lansdowne to Lamb, 31 Aug. 1827 (B.L., Wellesley papers, Add. MS 37305, f. 163).
111 Lamb to Landsdowne, 19 Sept. 1827 (ibid, f. 173).
112 Gower to Peel, 18 Dec. 1828 (B.L., Peel papers, Add. MS 40336, f. 173).
113 Peel to Gower, 26 Dec. 1828 (ibid, Add. Ms 40336, f. 187).
114 Ibid.
115 Gower to Peel, 15 Oct. 1829 (B.L., Peel papers, Add. MS 40337, f. 208).
116 Peel to Gower, 23 Nov. 1829 (P.R.O., HO 100/245).
117 Stanley to Crawford, 24 Jan 1831 (P.R.O.N.I., William Sharman Crawford papers, D856/D/13)
118 A Bill to repeal all the provisions of several acts relating to the presentments of money for public purposes, by grand juries in Ireland, and to make more effectual provisions relating to such presentments, H.C. 1831, Public Bills ii, 55.

119 *Hansard 3*, xv, 955 (19 Feb. 1833).
120 Ibid., 963 (O'Connell), 964 (Lefroy).
121 *Northern Whig*, 25 Feb. 1833.
122 *Belfast Newsletter*, 1 Mar. 1833.
123 *Hansard 3*, xix, 561–570 (11 July 1833), Bill to amend the laws relating to grand juries in Ireland as amended by the committee . . . , H.C. 1833, Public Bills ii, 633.
124 *Kilkenny Journal*, 17 Aug. 1833.
125 A Bill for consolidating and amending the laws relating to the presentment of public money by grand juries in Ireland, H.C. 1836, Public Bills iv, 49.
126 *Strabane Morning Post*, 19 July 1836.
127 6 & 7 Will. IV c.116.
128 Amendments to be proposed by Mr W.S. O'Brien, H.L. 1836, Public Bills iv, 133.
129 *Hansard 3*, xxxiv, 680 (21 June 1836)
130 *Hansard 3*, xxxvi, 423–425 (10 Feb. 1837).
131 *Report on the Irish grand jury laws made by a committee of the County Down Grand Jury appointed at the assizes of 1830*, amongst papers of the grand jury of County Antrim (P.R.O.N.I., Grand jury records, ANT/4/7/4).
132 *Report of the select committee appointed to inquire into the duties, salaries and fees of officers paid by counties in Ireland, and into presentments compulsory upon grand juries there and to report their opinion thereon . . .*, H.C. 1836 (527), xii, 3–8.
133 *Special report by W.P. O'Brien to the lord lieutenant upon the local government and taxation of Ireland, made in pursuance of the report of the select committee of the house of commons dated 20th July 1877*, [C 1965], H.C. 1878, xxiii, 765.
134 For a fuller discussion of the work of poor law boards see below, pp 70–71.
135 *Report of the royal commission on the poor laws and relief of distress: report on Ireland*, [C 4630], H.C. 1909, xxxviii, 20; W.F. Bailey, *Local and Central Government in Ireland. A sketch of the existing systems* (London, 1888), p. 31.
136 *First report of the select committee on grand jury presentments, Ireland*, H.C. 1822 (353), vii, 1; *Report of the commissioners appointed to revise the several laws under or by virtue of which monies are now raised by gand jury presentments in Ireland*, H.C. 1842 (386), xxiv, 15; P.J. Meghen, 'The Administrative Work of the Grand Jury', *Administration*, 6 (1958–59), 264.
137 46 & 47 Vict. c.43.
138 County Sligo Grand Jury Resolution Book, 1836–71 (N.L.I., MS 12,912, p. 16).
139 See for example *Morning Post*, 19 June 1865.
140 *Special report by W.P. O'Brien to the lord lieutenant upon the local government and taxation of Ireland*, [C 1965], H.C. 1878, xxiii, 713.
141 S. O'Cinneide, *A Law for the Poor* (Dublin, 1970), p. 106, quoted in Helen Burke, *The People and the Poor Law in 19th Century Ireland* (Littlehampton, 1987), p. 134; Burke, *The People and the Poor Law*, p. 155.
142 [J.W. Doyle, Bishop of Kildare and Leighlin], *Letters on the State of Ireland, by J.K.L.* (Dublin, 1825), p. 105.
143 Anglesey to Grey, 15 Jan. 1831 (P.R.O.N.I., Anglesey papers, D619/28C, f. 39).
144 Anglesey to Grey, 15 Apr. 1831 (ibid., D619/28C, f. 96).
145 R.B. McDowell, 'Ireland on the eve of the Famine', in R.D. Edwards and T.D. Williams (eds), *The Great Famine* (Dublin, 1956), pp 42–49; Helen Burke, *The People and the Poor Law*, pp 17–50; Christine Kinealy, 'The Poor Law during the Great Famine: An Administration in Crisis', in E.M. Crawford, *Famine: the Irish Experience 900–1900* (Edinburgh, 1989), pp 157–175.
146 Peter Grey, 'British Politics and the Ireland Question, 1843–1850', Ph.D. thesis (Cambridge, 1992).
147 *Hansard 3*, xxxvi, 465, 455 (13 Feb. 1837).

148 *Hansard 3*, xl, 780 (5 Feb. 1838).
149 *Special report by W.P. O'Brien to the lord lieutenant upon the local government and taxation of Ireland,* [C 1965], H.C. 1878, xxiii, 717. See also, Gerard O'Brien, 'The establishment of poor-law unions in Ireland, 1838–43', *Irish Historical Studies,* xxiii, no. 90 (Nov. 1982), 97–120.
150 6 and 7 Vict. c.92; W.L. Feingold, *The Revolt of the Tenantry: the transformation of local government in Ireland 1872-86* (Boston, 1984), p. 16.
151 McDowell, 'Ireland on the eve of the Famine', p. 50; Cormac O Grada, *The Great Irish Famine* (London, 1989), p. 31.
152 *A return of dates on which and the places where military and police have been employed in enforcing the collection of poor rates in Ireland, between the 1st January 1843 and the 1st January 1844,* H.C. 1844 (186), xl, 785.
153 *Report of the royal commission on the poor laws and relief of distress: report on Ireland,* [C.4630], H.C. 1909, xxxviii, 14.
154 McDowell, 'Ireland on the eve of the Famine', p. 52.
155 *Hansard 3*, lxv, 510 (22 July 1842).
156 The following discussion concentrates on Administrative developments during and after the Famine. Readers seeking information about the Famine itself, and its devastating human consequences, should consult Cecil Woodham-Smith, *The Great Hunger: Ireland 1845–49* (London, 1962); Mary E. Daly, *The Famine in Ireland* (Dublin, 1986); Cormac O Grada, *The Great Irish Famine* (London, 1989).
157 Kinealy, 'The Poor Law during the Great Famine', p. 160.
158 10 Vict. c.31.
159 In 1848 the number of unions was increased from 130 to 163 and the number of electoral divisions from 2,049 to 3,438. *Special report by W.P. O'Brien to the lord lieutenant upon the local government and taxation of Ireland,* [C 1965], H.C. 1878, xxiii, 715.
160 Daly, *The Famine in Ireland*, p. 94.
161 T.P. O'Neill, 'The Organization and Administration of Relief, 1845–52', in R.D. Edwards and T.D. Williams, *The Great Famine* (Dublin, 1956), p. 247.
162 Kinealy, 'The Poor Law during the Great Famine', p. 166, Daly, *The Famine in Ireland*, p. 97.
163 J. Grant, 'The Great Famine and the poor law in Ulster: the rate-in-aid issue of 1849', *Irish Historical Studies*, xxvii (May 1990), 30–47.
164 *Report of the royal commission on the poor laws and relief of distress: report on Ireland,* [C.4630], H.C. 1909, xxxviii, 18–19.
165 Kinealy, 'The Poor Law during the Great Famine', p. 168.
166 See below, p. 36.
167 *Special report by W.P. O'Brien to the lord lieutenant upon the local government and taxation of Ireland,* [C 1965], H.C. 1878, xxiii, 719.
168 Burke, *The People and the Poor Law*, pp 252–256.
169 *Special report by W.P. O'Brien to the lord lieutenant upon the local government and taxation of Ireland,* [C 1965], H.C. 1878, xxiii, 720; Burke, *The People and the Poor Law*, pp 274–5.
170 *Special report by W.P. O'Brien to the lord lieutenant upon the local government and taxation of Ireland,* [C 1965], H.C. 1878, xxiii, 719–720; Burke, *The People and the Poor Law*, pp 275–278.
171 Graham to Eaton, 22 Sept. 1876 (P.R.O.N.I., Boards of guardians records, BG15/B/1, p. 195).
172 Circular from poor law commission, 5 Dec. 1866 (ibid., BG14/O/1).
173 *Special report by W.P. O'Brien to the lord lieutenant upon the local government and taxation of Ireland,* [C 1965], H.C. 1878, xxiii, 724–5.
174 *Report of the royal commission on the poor laws and relief of distress: report on Ireland,* [C.4630], H.C. 1909, xxxviii, 53–55.

175 *Irish Times*, 4 Sept. 1897.
176 Minutes of meeting on 11 Nov. 1885 (P.R.O.N.I., Boards of guardians records, BG15/A/69, p. 127).
177 *Report of the royal commission on the poor laws and relief of distress: report on Ireland*, [C.4630], H.C. 1909, xxxviii, 20, *Special report by W.P. O'Brien to the lord lieutenant upon the local government and taxation of Ireland*, [C 1965], H.C. 1878, xxiii, 761; *Irish Times*, 3 Sept. 1897.
178 35 & 36 Vict. c.69.
179 Blakely to Reilly, 17 Sept. 1839 (P.R.O.N.I., Downshire papers, D671/C/12/734).
180 Gerard O'Brien, 'The establishment of poor-law unions in Ireland, 1838–43', *Irish Historical Studies*, xxiii, no. 90 (Nov. 1982), 108–112.
181 Carew to Clarendon, n.d. [Mar. 1848] (Bodleian Library, Clarendon papers [Irish], Box 8).
182 Feingold, *The Revolt of the tenantry*, p. 235.
183 Ibid., pp 85–87.
184 Ibid., p. 218.
185 Ibid., pp 168–9.
186 Thomas Nelson, *The Land War in County Kildare* (Maynooth, 1985), pp 19–25.
187 *Hansard 4*, liii, 558–563 (21 July 1898).
188 Report of J. McGlinny, 28 Mar. 1890 (S.P.O., Crime branch (special) files, S.26).
189 Armstrong to Montgomery, 9 Dec. 1893 (P.R.O.N.I., Montgomery papers, D627/428/227).
190 Feingold, *The Revolt of the Tenantry*, p. 234.
191 *Hansard 4*, xxxvii, 1449 (2 Mar. 1896).
192 *Hansard 4*, xxxvii, 629–632 (18 Feb. 1896).
193 Women's Association of Poor Law Guardians, fifteenth annual report, 1897, p. 7; sixteenth annual report, 1898, p. 14.
194 Anna Haslam, 'Irishwomen and the Local Government Act', *The Englishwoman's Review*, no. 239 (15 Oct. 1898).
195 Women's Association of Poor Law Guardians, seventeenth annual report, 1899, p. 9.
196 Ibid., p. 10.
197 Susanne R. Day, *The Amazing Philanthropists* (London, 1916).
198 Ibid., p. 104.
199 Stephen Brown and Desmond Clarke, *Ireland in Fiction: a guide to Irish novels, tales, romances and folklore, vol. 2* (Cork, 1985), p. 66.

SECTION II:

Local Government in Urban Areas
A. Town Commissioners

In the years immediately following the union, urban government in Ireland was limited to towns governed either by municipal corporations or under private acts of parliament. Inhabitants of towns without any urban authority could petition parliament for a private act to establish a body of commissioners authorised to undertake certain specified functions such as cleaning and lighting the streets, but this was a complicated and expensive process and it was often difficult to secure the necessary level of support amongst local householders. A proposal in 1811 to establish town commissioners in Newry, County Down, provoked strong opposition within the town. The plan would have provided for twenty-three commissioners to regulate the pilotage of the harbour and to provide street lighting, a town watch and a fire service. Opponents saw it as a means of securing political influence and patronage for the sponsor, Lord Kilmorey. Describing to Lord Downshire the steps taken to defeat the bill, Thomas Greer remarked that it would have created thirty to forty jobs, including a treasurer and a secretary to the commissioners, constables, watchmen, firemen, inspectors, a prison keeper, a lamp contractor, a harbour master, a pilot officer and a surveyor. Greer and others set themselves to 'exposing the cloven foot for the good of the town', and managed to stir up popular resistance to such an extent that a meeting to approve the bill was adjourned without a vote and the measure abandoned.[1] The continued absence of any town authority proved detrimental to the town, and the poor state of the streets and inadequate water supply threatened to damage trade. In 1824 another attempt was made to submit a bill to parliament, this time sponsored not only by Kilmorey but also by Samuel Reid, one of the leading opponents of the previous measure. This time a body of twenty-one commissioners was proposed, twelve of whom were to be elected, the others comprising the Earl of Kilmorey and his agent, Lord Downshire and his agent, the local MP, seneschal, vicar and church wardens, all of whom were connected with Kilmorey either through patronage or political allegiance. This bill also was widely opposed and was rejected by parliament.[2] Four years later an act was passed establishing twenty-one commissioners of police in Newry, to be elected annually with powers to raise a rate for the purpose of watching and lighting the streets. This act became, in the words of a recent historian of the town, 'the model for municipal administration throughout Ireland', for it formed the basis of legislation passed in July 1828 empowering any borough in which basic services (lighting, watching, cleansing, paving) were not provided to elect commissioners for this purpose.[3] All inhabitants of houses rated at £5 or more within the town or within one mile of its boundaries were entitled to vote at a public meeting on whether or not to adopt the act. If the meeting decided to go ahead, commissioners numbering not less than nine or more than twenty-one were to be elected from amongst residents rated at £20 or more. The commissioners were to go out of office every three years, though individuals could be re-elected. They were to meet on the first Monday of every month at noon and were to keep minutes of their proceedings. As a body the commissioners were empowered to levy a rate on all property with more than £5 yearly value and to use the funds raised to provide a variety of services. These included lighting, cleaning and paving the streets, constructing sewers and drains, digging wells and providing for pumped water, and keeping a fire engine. Ratepayers could adopt the provisions of the act for any one or more of these purposes as they saw fit. Contracts made by the commissioners were not valid for more than three years and no-one serving as a commissioner was to have an interest in any contract. The commissioners were to keep yearly accounts, which were to be made available to any rate-payer who wished to see them.

A total of sixty-six towns adopted the act in the succeeding decades, from Ballymoney in County Antrim to Bandon in County Cork.[4] The experience of towns under the act varied. Many adopted only a limited portion of its provisions in order to reduce the burden on ratepayers. Writing to James Cramsie, a leading figure in Ballymoney, in 1845 to remind him that a meeting was to take place on 3 March concerning the cleansing and lighting of the town, Thomas Davison commented that popular feeling was in favour of carrying the act into execution, 'but there will likely be opposition as to the lighting on account of the expense'.[5] Tipperary town commission, which was constituted in 1833, initially assumed responsibility simply for cleaning the town.[6] Commissioners who attempted to take a more active role found themselves hampered not only by the parsimony of ratepayers but also by the provisions of the act itself. Under clause 54 of the act, for example, sewers and drains could be constructed but the cost had to be defrayed out of the rates, which were barely sufficient in most cases for ordinary purposes. There was no provision for a special sewer rate. Provision for the supply of water was limited to a power to dig wells and erect pumps in the streets but not to undertake more extensive work.

More extensive powers of town management were conferred on commissioners by an act passed in 1854.[7] This was intended to enable towns to avail themselves of the provisions of the towns improvement clauses acts passed in 1847 for England and Wales, without going to the expense of private legislation. Any town, including those which already had either a municipal corporation or town commissioners, could adopt the act at a public meeting of ratepayers rated at £8 and above, subject to the approval of the lord lieutenant. In corporate towns, the town council or municipal board automatically became the commissioners. In other places commissioners were to be elected from amongst ratepayers valued at £12 and over. The act provided for a broadly-based electorate encompassing all those house-holders whose premises were rated under the poor law at £4 or above, together with lessors of property valued at £50 or over who resided within five miles of the town's boundaries. Rating under the act itself was to be uniform rather than graduated as under the old act. The extent to which the new act proved superior to that of 1828 is indicated by the fact that by 1878 all but eleven of the sixty-six towns which had adopted the earlier act had given this up in favour of the 1854 act. (The eleven were Tralee, Armagh, Mallow, Bandon, Youghal, Dungannon, Omagh, Monaghan, Downpatrick, Wicklow and Fethard.) Commissioners elected under the act of 1854 could arrange for the construction of a new sewer at the expense of the district, borrowing money for the purpose and spreading repayment over thirty years. They could also take steps to procure a better water supply and levy an additional 6d in the pound on the rates for the purpose. The limits of rating were fixed at 1s 6d in the £ where the power to supply water was adopted and 1s in other cases. (An upper limit of 2s replaced that of 1s 6d in 1874 under the public health act of that year.) Commissioners could erect public baths and wash-houses and provide and maintain places of public recreation. Their accounts, which were to be audited by two auditors appointed by ratepayers, were to be made up one month before the annual general meeting in June, and were to remain open to inspection by ratepayers without charge. Previously commissioners were merely required to print their accounts once a year. Expenditure in towns which adopted the act was mainly devoted to such items as street cleaning and lighting, water supply, sewerage, sanitary expenses, salaries, printing and stationery. Amounts raised on the rates were relatively small. The Ballymoney town commissioners, for example, levied a rate of 1s in the £ for the year 1858–9, producing a sum of £172 6s 10d. The main items of expenditure which appeared in the commissioners' accounts for the year were sweeping and improving the streets, insuring the town hall, contracting with the Ballymoney Gas Company to light, extinguish and keep clean the public lamps, and the construction of new footpaths.[8]

One of the first towns to adopt the new act was Lurgan in County Armagh. The first annual report of the Lurgan commissioners, published in 1856, described their 'unremitting exertions' to promote the health and cleanliness of the town. In the course of the year they had caused seventeen cellars and 'forty-four pestilent dung-pits' to be closed and fifty-two additional privies to be built. They had sunk a new well in the high street and erected two new pumps. They had had three ruinous buildings removed and three repaired, had made a new clothes market and improved the appearance of the mall, had erected ten new gas lamps presented to the town by Lord Lurgan and had made arrangements for the establishment of a telegraph office. They regarded their chief work, however, to have been the formation of a new north-east sewer, built of brick and flushed with water drawn from Lord Lurgan's lake. This replaced a 'foul drain' which had previously polluted the valley separating the town from Lord Lurgan's domain. Two years earlier the poor law commissioners had called on the guardians of Lurgan poor law union to remedy the situation, and the sanitary committee of the board had handed the matter over to the town commissioners at the first opportunity. Lord Lurgan, who was chairman of the town commissioners, had provided the necessary funds to build the sewer and an additional rate had been levied on the north-eastern district to repay the loan. It is clear from the report that not all the inhabitants of the town welcomed the improvement. Only £5 2s 1d, we are told, remained unpaid of the £53 8s 3d assessed on the district, showing that those objecting to the work on the grounds that the area was already sufficiently well drained were a very small minority, 'but as a great deal of misrepresentation has been circulated on this question, the commissioners have felt called upon to go into the matter at greater length than would otherwise have been necessary'. The report concluded with the self-congratulatory observation that while the cleanliness and sanitation of the town had been much improved, the commissioners had not found it necessary to levy higher rates, the general purposes rate being 8d in the £, and 1s 1d in the £ in the district of the sewer, compared to a previous rate of around 1s in the £.[9] Over the following years much space in the annual reports was taken up with the problems caused by the scarcity of water in Lurgan and the necessity of procuring an adequate supply. In 1858 the professor of engineering at the Queen's College, Belfast, Professor Thompson, prepared a report containing two schemes for supplying the town, both of which would have necessitated the establishment of a joint stock company to undertake the work, charging consumers for water in the same way as the gas company. Rate-payers would have had to meet the cost of fire plugs, watering places for animals and water carts for cleaning the streets. Despite serious fires in the town in 1859 and 1863, attempts to launch a water supply company, with funds being provided both by the commissioners and by Lord Lurgan himself, foundered when insufficient numbers of shares were taken up.[10] The support of a leading landowner was immensely valuable in undertaking works of improvement. Lurgan town commission benefited greatly from the energy and resources of Lord Lurgan, who owned most of the town. Commenting on the state of the town in 1877, the commissioners appointed to inquire into the local government and taxation of towns commended it as an example of 'good and successful management, . . . greatly owing to the personal attention to the interests of the town and its inhabitants given by Lord Lurgan, and his agent, Mr Hancocks, who have both taken an active part in the municipal administration as town commissioners'.[11] Lisburn in County Down was similarly fortunate, being 'much indebted to the liberality of the present owner, Sir Richard Wallace, and his predecessor, the late Lord Hertford'. It was, apparently, one of the few towns in which an effective fire brigade was maintained by the town commissioners. [12]

The existence of a body of town commissioners was no guarantee of satisfactory municipal administration. The report of the select committee on local government in towns, which appeared in 1878, noted that town commissioners in both Mallow and Killarney had practically abdicated their functions. Those in Mallow had done nothing since 1841 and the salaries of officials were twelve years in arrears.[13] Appearing before the select committee on local government the previous year, Leopold Cust, a magistrate of Tipperary, stated that municipal administration had broken down in Tipperary town due to a lack of independent men coming forward to act as commissioners. Those who did serve, Cust maintained, were unduly influenced by a fear of the mob, and he cited the crowding of the streets by butchers' stalls as evidence of this.

> I have even seen calves killed in the streets and hanging up dead; the Commissioners would not dare to interfere; I know that the present chairman has resigned, and I believe he does not make it a secret to say one of the chief difficulties which he had to contend with was the removal of those stalls. He knew at once that if he attempted to remove them there would be difficulties interposed against their removal, and probably personal danger to himself.

Tipperary had not adopted the act of 1854 until 1875, three earlier attempts to adopt the act having failed to achieve the necessary support. According to Cust many 'respectable men' (by which he meant wealthy merchants) had put themselves forward for election to the new body of commissioners,

> but the day before [the election] a green placard appeared, saying, that So-and-So were to be the elect of the people, and So-and-So were elected, and respectable men, representing the wealth and intelligence of the town who had come forward were not, with some few exceptions, of course.

The 'green placard' was, he explained, widely spoken of as a Fenian placard. Raising the property qualification for commissioners would not remedy the situation, Cust believed, as the town was so small that this would simply mean that the same people served as commissioners over and over again, as had happened under the 1828 act:

> a certain body of men got the thing into their own hands, and they used to go on electing men who they knew would not act, on purpose to keep it in their own hands. The chairman was a man in the position of a feather and bone merchant, and the whole thing became a farce.[14]

The only solution in Cust's opinion was for the government to appoint paid commissioners. When the select committee came to issue its final report the following year, it referred to the importance of securing a proper representation on governing bodies of wealthier and more educated rate-payers, and recommended that owners and occupiers should vote separately, each group electing its own representatives. If town commissioners were drawn more from the ranks of leading townsmen, the report argued, it might be possible to entrust them with wider functions and to lift the statutory limits on rating powers.[15] Much of the concern expressed about the social status of town commissioners was politically motivated, as Cust's comments about 'a green placard' indicate. Town commissioners drawn from the wealthier and more educated classes were more likely to be conservative (and protestant) and as such were regarded as less liable to indulge in extravagant expenditure or to be swayed by sectional interests. The idea of providing separate representation for property-holders, however, appeared increasingly anachronistic against the background of an expanding parliamentary franchise. In 1880 the qualification for membership of town bodies was reduced rather than increased, when by an act of that year all voters became eligible for membership.[16]

Public health legislation passed in the second half of the nineteenth century invested town authorities with new statutory responsibilities. The burial grounds act of 1856, for example, had made town commissioners burial boards under the act, while the public health act of 1866 laid certain statutory responsibilities upon them with regard to the provision of sewers and removal of nuisances. In order to ensure that these responsibilities were met, the lord lieutenant (later the local government board) was empowered, where any sewer or nuisance authority was found to be in default, to set a time limit within which work was to be carried out and then to appoint someone to execute it at the expense of the defaulting authority. Under the public health act of 1874, towns with populations of over 6,000 were created urban sanitary districts and their town commissioners urban sanitary authorities with the power to set an unlimited rate for sanitary purposes. Forty towns were constituted sanitary districts following this act, eleven corporate towns, sixteen towns which which had adopted the town improvement act of 1854 and thirteen which were under local acts or that of 1828. In smaller towns the board of guardians of the poor law union incorporating the town acted as the sanitary authority.[17] That these acts did help to stir municipal authorities into action is indicated by expenditure levels in the period after 1866. Town commissioners in the twenty-nine towns which were constituted urban sanitary districts (excluding corporate towns) spent a total of £174,549 in 1876 compared with £100,528 in 1866.[18] Concluding their survey of the local government of towns in 1877, the commission of inquiry noted considerable improvements in the sanitary condition of towns since the passage of the public health act, but observed that much remained to be done. Few towns possessed a proper sewage system or water supply while in some, such as Ennis, Bray and Queenstown, the commissioners had been shocked by what they described as 'an almost culpable degree of apathy on the part of the sanitary authority and the inhabitants generally'. In Ennis, for example, they reported a

> marked distinction between the attention paid to the cleansing and scavenging of the richer and poorer parts of the town, but scarcely any of the houses have a closet, privy or other accommodation, and after night-fall the streets are in such a state . . . that it becomes a question along which foot-passengers can most safely walk. The sewerage is utterly defective and insufficient, and the water supply almost nil.[19]

But generally speaking they accepted that some allowance should be made for 'a reluctance to press too hardly on individuals', bearing in mind that to carry out all the recommendations of the sanitary officers without regard to expense or local circumstances would create such a degree of opposition to the sanitary act 'as to imperil its usefulness'.[20]

One of the problems identified both by the commission of inquiry into the local government and taxation of towns in 1877, and by the select committee on the same subject which reported the following year, was the existence of a number of different authorities all executing administrative responsibilities and levying separate rates within town boundaries. In many towns responsibility for certain roads and public works was vested in the grand jury of the county or

in the grand jury of the town itself in the case of urban boroughs such
as Waterford and Kilkenny. There could be three different authorities
within one town, the town commissioners, the board of guardians and
the grand jury. In some places four authorities were involved, the
town commissioners, the board of guardians and two grand juries. The
suburb of Graigue, for example, which formed part of the borough of
Carlow, lay in the Queen's County, while the rest of the town was part
of County Carlow. The resulting division of responsibility was an
obstacle to improvement. Graigue was one of the poorest districts of
Carlow town and at the time of the commission of inquiry lacked any
main sewers. The cost of constructing a sewer would have fallen on
both the town commissioners and the grand jury of the Queen's
County, which was responsible for repairing streets and footpaths in
the district. The grand jury refused to defray any portion of the
expense of main sewers out of the county cess, maintaining that the
onus lay on the town commissioners as the urban sanitary authority.[21]
The double taxation to which many towns were subject had long been
a source of grievance amongst residents, who resented having to pay
both county cess and town rates. It was also felt to be one reason why
more towns had not adopted the town improvement act of 1854.[22] A
number of towns and cities took steps to relieve themselves from
grand jury assessments by taking over responsibility for roads, bridges
and the like within their own boundaries, but this could only be done
by means of a special act of parliament. Belfast, Newry, Enniskillen,
Londonderry, Galway, Dungarvan, Queenstown, Sligo and the five
principal townships of County Dublin managed by means of local acts
to charge themselves with the upkeep of their own roads, whilst con-
tinuing to contribute towards grand jury expenses in respect of
county-at-large expenditure such as the upkeep of prisons and lunatic
asylums. Wexford achieved the same object by means of a provisional
order under the provisions of the local government act of 1872, which
enabled governing bodies of towns to take on new powers without
having to go to the expense of a private act of parliament. The 1872
act empowered the local government board, which took over immediate responsibility for the government of towns and the adminstration of the poor law and the sanitary laws from the viceroy and the
chief secretary, to respond to petitions from local bodies by inquiring
into the matter and, where the inquiry proved satisfactory, granting
the petition by provisional order. In this way town authorities could
obtain powers to purchase land for public use, to incorporate adjoin-
ing districts into the main body of the town, to authorise the making
of a rate in addition to the existing maximum, to execute, amend or
repeal any local act, to extend borrowing powers in certain cases, and
to transfer to the governing body of the town from the grand jury all

responsibility for roads, bridges, footpaths and public works and all relevant taxation.[23] In 1873 parliament approved a provisional order granted by the local government board transferring exclusive authority over roads and bridges to Wexford town council from the grand jury of the county. Similar applications were made by Westport and Ballina in County Mayo, Belturbet in County Cavan and Newtownards in County Down. In these cases, however, the grand juries refused to consent to the transfer and since their consent was required under the act, the board was unable to grant the orders. The board was clearly unhappy with the situation, questioning in its annual report for 1874

> why the consent of the grand jury was made a necessary preliminary, as it was most natural that the body which it was proposed to deprive of its jurisdiction and its power of taxation should object to the proposal, however beneficial it might be to the parties residing in the district which petitioned to be disannexed'.[24]

The provisional order procedure was, nevertheless, extensively used by town authorities and the annual reports of the local government board record the numerous orders approved each year. Many of these were applications from towns of less than 6,000 inhabitants to be constituted an urban sanitary district, thus enabling the town commissioners to take over responsibility for sanitary matters from the poor law guardians. In 1887, for example, the town commissioners of Ballymoney petitioned the local government board to be made the sanitary authority for the town, which had a population of around 3,000 people. Of the fifty-eight guardians of the Ballymoney poor law union (twenty-nine elected, twenty-nine ex officio) only six, three elected and three ex officio, were resident within the town, and the sanitary affairs of the district were generally left in the hands of the three elected guardians. If the commissioners were constituted an urban sanitary authority, the management of affairs would, they argued, be under the control of a larger number of people who would be better acquainted with the circumstances and requirements of the district. An opportunity had also arisen to purchase an interest in the markets of Ballymoney which, the commissioners explained, they wished to seize as this would give them the power to make bye-laws and generally improve the regulation of the markets and the transaction of business. But in order to purchase the interest the commissioners needed the power to raise the sum required, and this they could only do as an urban sanitary authority.[25] An order constituting the town of Ballymoney an urban sanitary district was granted the following year.[26]

By the end of the century the legislation governing the administration of towns was badly in need of consolidation. The situation whereby seventy-seven towns were governed under the town improvement act of 1854 (including five which were also municipal corporations) while a further eleven remained under the act of 1828, was clearly anomalous, while the existence of overlapping authorities and jurisdictions continued to hamper efficient administration. Individual town bodies varied both in terms of their powers and their efficiency, what they shared was a directly elected membership. This was a crucial factor in preserving them from the kind of concerted public criticism that was directed at the unreformed municipal corporations in the decades before 1840,[27] and, in the competition between town councils and grand juries for administrative authority and taxing powers in urban districts, the unrepresentative nature of grand juries weakened their position. Reporting on a deputation of town commissioners to the viceroy in 1865 to request that townships should be relieved from grand jury assessments, the *Morning Post* commented that the real problem was the grand jury system itself, which was founded on a divorce of taxation from representation.[28] The strength of town councils in this respect is evident in the shape of local government reform in 1898, for while the structure of county administration underwent a radical alteration in that year, urban adminstration, as we shall see, remained little changed.

Local Government in Urban Areas
B. Municipal Corporations

The report of the commissioners appointed to inquire into municipal corporations in Ireland, published in 1835, merely confirmed what most people already suspected, that Irish corporations had long ceased to pay any attention to the interests or welfare of the inhabitants of Irish cities and towns but devoted their energies to protecting the position of a narrow political and sectarian class. The original intention in establishing corporations was to benefit the residents of corporate districts and residents were intended to be identified in interest with the members of the corporation. As they developed, however, the interests of Irish corporations, most of which were self-perpetuating oligarchies, became divorced from those of residents. In only one corporation, that of Tuam, were the majority of the governing body catholic. 'The unpopular character of municipal bodies is thus, in too many cases', the commissioners concluded,

> aggravated by their being considered inimical, on the ground of sectarian feelings, to a great majority of the resident population, and they become instrumental to the continuance of the unhappy dissensions which it has so long been the policy of the legislature to allay.[29]

The commissioners identified four main defects in the system of municipal government, the power of self-election which rested in governing bodies, the absolute control vested in them respecting admission to the corporate franchise, the tendency to dispense with any residence qualification for members and officers, and the exclusion of the inhabitants at large from any effective voice in the management of local affairs and the expenditure of local funds.[30]

In the course of their enquiries, the commissioners took detailed evidence concerning the sixty corporations then existing, from Ardee in County Louth to Youghal in County Cork. Every aspect of corporate government was looked at, beginning with the charter and constitution of each corporation and moving on through its activities, property, and income. Each corporation was different, but few came well out of the inquiry. In the town of Galway, for example, the management of corporate affairs was found to be in the hands of a select, self-electing body from which many 'respectable citizens' were excluded.

> It has been for many years under the patronage and influence of James Daly, Esq., of Dunsandle, and his family; at whose nomination the principal corporate officers appear to have long been elected by the common council, and for the forty years preceding 1817 the name of Daly alone occurs in the list of mayors . . . The effect has been, to place the corporation in opposition to a large proportion of the inhabitants, and the general state and prosperity of the town appear to have suffered from their mutual jealousies and disunion.[31]

Extravagance and improvidence had reduced the corporation of Londonderry to a state of insolvency. This, in the opinion of the commissioners, was due less to private misconduct than to the character of the corporate body, which was again self-elective and thus free from public scrutiny. Most members of the governing body, which was exclusively protestant, were non-resident and few were connected with the trading interests of the town. The corporation became insolvent in 1831, demonstrating 'the total incompetence of such a body to discharge, efficiently and usefully, the duties of public trustees or the functions of municipal government'. A private act passed in 1832 had created a police committee for Londonderry consisting of the mayor and twelve inhabitants chosen annually by rate-payers valued at £20 and above, and empowered to execute powers with regard to lighting the city with gas, paving the streets and making sewers. This act did not, the commissioners felt, work very well but it did at least establish the principle of giving rate-payers a say in the management of their own municipal affairs.[32] Tuam in County Galway provided a rare example of a town in which the corporation had some pretensions to a popular character. The corporation consisted of a sovereign, twelve free burgesses and two sergeants at mace. At the period of the Union the borough had been under the patronage of the Honorable Walter Yelverton and John Lord Clanmorris but had since the union, when it lost the privilege of returning MPs, become independent. In 1811 the entire body of burgesses voluntarily changed and in 1835 all the burgesses, with one exception, were catholic. 'It was stated to us', the commissioners noted, 'that there are not now any religious or political prejudices in the election of burgesses, but that within the last few years great efforts have been made by individual burgesses to have their own friends elected, in order to have a majority'. Corporate activities were extremely limited. There was no local police force, the town was not lighted or paved or watched and the streets were repaired under the authority of the grand jury. The main items of corporate expenditure were the salaries of officers, the rent of the Shambles and the fish market and the repair and upkeep of the market-house and town clock. In respect to the last two items the corporation was in debt to a former sovereign, Charles Blake.[33]

In two of the principal cities of Ireland, Dublin and Belfast, the corporations were found to be wholly inadequate. The corporation of Belfast comprised the lord of the castle, the sovereign and twelve burgesses nominated by the lord and holding their offices for life. Responsibility for municipal government had already been transferred to other bodies, the police commissioners, an elective body established in 1800, who were responsible for paving, lighting and cleaning the streets, and for providing a fire service and a night watch; the ballast board which was responsible for the management of the port and the Belfast Charitable Society, established in 1752 to provide relief for the destitute poor and which, under the Belfast police act of 1800, was responsible for the provision of water and the upkeep of the public graveyard.[34] In Dublin the corporate body comprised the lord mayor, two sheriffs, twenty-four aldermen elected for life from amongst those whose had served as sheriff (known as sheriffs' peers), and 144 common council men made up of forty-eight sheriffs' peers and ninety-six representatives of trades guilds. All of these were drawn from a body of around 4,000 hereditary freemen. The corporation was originally responsible for paving, cleansing and lighting the streets of the city but these duties were gradually devolved to other bodies, leaving the corporation itself, as the commissioners noted in their report, 'almost totally disconnected from the administration of the funds, and relieved from the performance of the trusts'.[35] Members of the corporation were thus able to devote themselves to the serious business of passing resolutions of loyalty to the crown and the viceroy. Unfortunately the new methods of administration adopted in Dublin did not prove entirely satisfactory. Commissioners appointed by the lord lieutenant in 1807 to look after the streets and to regulate the city's water supply and sewage system were later found to have been guilty of serious mismanagement and to have run up considerable debts. New commissioners were appointed in 1827.[36]

The report on Irish municipal corporations produced by the commissioners of inquiry was thorough and comprehensive, and its conclusion that a complete reform of municipal government was required was accepted by all parties. There was serious disagreement, however, over the shape which such a reform should take. The government's hand was to some extent forced by the measure reforming English municipal corporations introduced by the whig government in 1835, which established new borough councils in all the 178 existing boroughs in England and Wales to be elected by all ratepaying male householders. The bill for Ireland which was introduced in the commons in July 1835 by Louis Perrin, who had chaired the Irish commis-

sion, was more restrictive than its English counterpart but it still represented a major change in urban administration, based on the principle of local democracy. Under the bill municipal corporations were
to become fully elective, with a £10 householder franchise for towns
with populations of over 20,000 people and £5 in smaller towns. To
balance this, freemen, who were almost all protestant, retained their
municipal vote, and the lord lieutenant was given the power to
appoint borough magistrates, a power which had previously rested
with corporations. (During the committee stage of the bill's progress
through the commons the lord lieutenant was also given the appointment of sheriffs.) Reaction to the bill varied. Frederick Shaw, who sat
for Dublin University, condemned the measure as an attack on loyal
Irish protestants. Pointing out that the 'origin and principal use' of
Irish corporations was to secure the British connection and to encourage the protestant religion, he declared that

> while he would never set his face against real improvement, come from
> what quarter it might, he certainly would not be a consenting party to
> place the municipal authorities and local jurisdiction throughout Ireland
> in the hands of those whose avowed object was to subvert the Established
> Church in that country, and whose scarcely concealed motive was to sep-
> arate its institutions from Great Britain.[37]

Daniel O'Connell on the other hand welcomed the bill as a sign that
the days of corrupt corporations were numbered. Far from protecting
the British connection, the preservation of Irish corporations would
undermine it. The only means of maintaining the connection, he
insisted, 'is by allowing the Irish people to share the advantages of the
British institutions, and this it is proposed to do under the present
bill'. To O'Connell, municipal reform was a crucial step in completing
the process initiated by catholic emancipation and he hailed the bill as

> the commencement of the reign of Justice. . . . There remains this corpo-
> rate monopoly and it is the only thing remaining that prevents justice
> being done to the people. This, and this alone, shuts the inhabitants out
> from participation in the advantages of British institutions; and upon this
> question the government are prepared to give the people of Ireland
> redress.[38]

His belief in the importance of the measure, an importance which was
as much symbolic as practical, explains why he was prepared to accept
a greatly watered down version of the bill when opposition from the
lords threatened to kill it altogether.[39] Tory peers, who held a majority in the house of lords, were deeply hostile to any measure of reform
arguing that it would weaken the protestant ascendancy and having
little confidence in the fruits of democracy, but under pressure from
Peel they agreed to compromise and to accept a plan to give elective

councils to a limited number of large towns on a £10 (male) house-holder franchise.[40]

The final measure, which was not passed until 1840,[41] abolished the existing corporations, preserving borough councils in just ten places (Dublin, Cork, Limerick, Belfast, Londonderry, Drogheda, Kilkenny, Sligo, Waterford and Clonmel), though ratepayers in non-incorporated towns with populations of over 3,000 could petition the lord lieutenant for incorporation. (Wexford was incorporated in 1845.) The powers of the new councils were strictly defined – control of police, for example, was excluded – and limited in regard to matters such as taxation. A general power was conferred on corporations to make bye-laws, subject to the lord lieutenant's approval, for the good government of the borough and for the prevention or suppression of nuisances. The power to appoint magistrates and sheriffs was transferred to the lord lieutenant. (A later act, passed in 1876,[42] restored the nomination of sheriffs to municipal corporations, the lord lieutenant appointing from a list of three names submitted by the corporation.) Boroughs which lost their corporation were encouraged to adopt the paving and lighting act of 1828. Where they had already done so, any property belonging to the dissolved corporation was vested in the town commissioners. With regard to towns which had not adopted the act of 1828, the municipal reform act provided for the election of municipal commissioners (one for every 500 inhabitants) in towns where the annual value of corporate property exceeded £100. (Commissioners were duly elected in 19 towns, all of which, with the exception of Carrickfergus, subsequently adopted either the act of 1828 or the later town improvement act of 1854.) In towns where the annual value of corporate property was less than £100 it was vested in the poor law guardians, pending adoption of the act of 1828.

The corporate bodies created by the municipal reform act comprised a mayor, aldermen and councillors, the number of each of the latter categories being prescribed either by the act itself or in charters of incorporation granted afterwards. (Belfast, for example, was given a corporation of thirty councillors and ten aldermen, Kilkenny one of eighteen councillors and six aldermen.) To be eligible for office, candidates were required to be on the burgess roll (i.e. an adult man, resident in the borough or within seven miles of it for at least a year, who occupied property rated at not less than £10 p.a. and who was up to date with all rate payments) and possessed of property, real or personal, to the value of £1,000 over and above any debts, or to be the occupier of a house rated for poor law purposes at £25 p.a. One-third of the councillors were to go out of office each year, and one-half of the aldermen every three years. The quorum for council meetings was to be one-third of the whole, with matters being decided by majority vote. Councils were empowered to appoint committees to oversee particular aspects of council business, provided that their acts were submitted to the full council for approval. In the 1870s Waterford Corporation had committees meeting weekly to discuss finance, streets, waterworks and public health. In the opinion of the town clerk of Waterford, Joseph Howard, who appeared before the select committee on the local government and taxation of towns in 1877: 'practically it is the committees that do the work of the council'.[43]

Just how limited the 1840 act was became clear when, following the passage of the town improvements act in 1854, five of the eleven municipal corporations adopted the act (although in 1877, neither Clonmel nor Kilkenny was levying any rate under its provisions.)[44] Other corporations had initiated private improvement acts to enable them to undertake more extensive activities than those permitted under the act of 1840. In an article on Belfast urban government, Cornelius O'Leary has described how Belfast Corporation promoted improvement acts in 1845, 1846 and 1847 to enable it to borrow money in order to undertake projects which ranged from widening the streets to taking over the privately-owned gasworks and draining the Blackstaff river. The sums raised under these acts, amounting to over £200,000, were not, however, strictly applied to the purposes specified in the act (the corporation decided to purchase a site for a new central market, instead of buying out the gasworks) and in 1854 the corporation found itself in court charged with borrowing in excess of the amount authorised by the acts and of misapplying the money borrowed. Ruling on the case, the lord chancellor of Ireland, Maziere Brady, laid down that in relation to corporate property, corporations no longer acted as private individuals but as trustees and as such were liable to be called to account in the same manner as trustees of any charitable fund. He then found the allegations against the corporation proven. This case, O'Leary concludes, undoubtedly contributed to Belfast's unsavoury reputation as far as urban administration was concerned, but he emphasises the extent to which the conservative-held corporation was genuinely committed to urban improvement, overseeing the construction of new streets and the provision of a new, much-needed central market.[45] The corporation does not appear to have been deterred from undertaking major projects by its experience in the courts. Following the passage of the local government act of 1872, the corporation applied to the local government board for a provisional order extending its borrowing powers to £50,000 and granting powers of compulsory purchase in order to widen streets, erect public baths and wash-houses and create a 'people's garden'. The board instituted an inquiry to hear local objections, but since the petition had, according to the board, the almost unanimous support of the inhabtants, it was decided to grant the order, which was duly confirmed by parliament in 1873.[46] Reporting in 1878, the select committee on the local government of towns in Ireland gave the corporation a fairly clean bill of health. Reference was made to complaints concerning the corporation's neglect of the interests of the catholic population of the city, but general satisfaction was expressed with the way municipal affairs were managed.[47]

The 1878 select committee was more critical of Dublin Corporation, referring to slack attendance at meetings, inattention to important duties such as the condition of the streets and sanitary matters generally, and criticising a lack of proper control in dealing with officials and workmen.[48] This view was echoed by an inspector of the local government board in 1902 who criticised the corporation's excessive spending and financial mismanagement.[49] Contemporary criticism of the corporation was often directed as much against its political complexion as against its actions, or lack of them. This was true from the earliest years of the reformed corporation when O'Connell served as the first lord mayor. In his biography of O'Connell, Oliver MacDonagh argues that while O'Connell's critics ridiculed his delight in the trappings of the mayoralty, his period in the office (November 1841 to October 1842) was in fact one of efficient and impartial administration.[50] By the later decades of the century, the character of the corporation had taken on a more overtly nationalist hue as representatives of the city's business elite, who were predominantly conservative, were gradually replaced by members of lower status and income who were generally nationalists. Mary Daly notes that by 1890 one-third of the total members of the corporation were either grocers or publicans or both, and that whereas in the late 1850s the political balance of the corporation had been evenly split betweeen liberal and conservative, by 1896 the number of conservatives had been reduced to eleven members out of a total of sixty.[51] Members of the corporation used their position to raise political issues and to further political campaigns, from the disestablishment of the Church of Ireland in the 1860s to home rule in the 1880s. Unionists responded by seizing on instances of maladministration as a useful stick with which to beat the nationalists, for if the latter could not administer the capital efficiently, it was argued, how could they be entrusted with the country?

Dublin was regarded as the flagship as far as municipal government was concerned, but members of other corporations were equally determined that corporate decisions should take regard of wider political questions. At a monthly meeting of the Cork Municipal Council held in March 1870, Sir William Cardwell proposed that the council should pass a resolution urging that the military commander of the Cork district, Sir A. Cunynghame, should replace Lord Strathnairn, who was about to leave Ireland as the commander of the forces. This was opposed by the nationalist politician A.M. Sullivan, who proceeded to attack Strathnairn claiming that he had been sent 'from the bloody cannon's mouth in India . . . to be a military satrap of England in this country'.[52] Such incidents were characteristic of council meetings at this time. Giving evidence to the select committee on the local government of towns in 1877, William Verling Gregg, who had been elected to the Cork City Council in 1850, and had sat as an alderman for the previous sixteen years, observed that a political and religious element was too often introduced to council discussions.

> I happen to be one of the unfortunate minority in the council, and it is sometimes not a very pleasant thing to have to be getting up to oppose these matters which are introduced, and take up a very considerable time; we have too much oratory there entirely.[53]

Gregg also commented on the alteration that had taken place in the composition of the council since he had first become a member. A great many of the 'respectable' citizens who had formally been members had retired and had not been replaced. Since the introduction of working men to the council, 'citizens of the first class no longer consider it an honour to be on the council'. He nevertheless stressed that the present members were both respectable and intelligent – there were, he said, 'some very good working men in the council'[54] – an opinion which many of his conservative colleagues do not appear to have shared. Henry Young, who had been a member of the council from 1854 until 1868, complained that members no longer represented the wealth and intelligence of the city. When he had retired in 1868 there had been twelve magistrates, one deputy lieutenant and three members of parliament on the council. In 1877 there were just five magistrates. Young's real complaint, however, seems to have been that the great majority of councillors were Liberals who approved expenditure on items such as the O'Connell centenary.[55]

Government ministers regarded the growing influence of Irish nationalists on local councils with some apprehension, and council elections were monitored by the police who reported on the results to Dublin Castle. But, as such reports make clear, politics was not always in the forefront of the minds of the electorate. Following the municipal election in Limerick in 1896, Head Constable John Morrow informed his superior that there had been only one contest, between an out-going councillor, Major M.J. Kenny, and J.O. Moylan, a retired school teacher who had been put forward by the local ratepayers association. Kenny defeated his rival by forty-two votes to twenty-one, despite having changed his political allegiance from federalist to unionist. According to Morrow, Kenny was 'a very popular gentleman' who was secretary to the Greenpark race committee and to the horseshow committee, as well as being a friend of and assistant to Mr Ellard, the clerk of the crown and peace. In addition to these recommendations, he had the support of the trades and labour council.[56]

In general it would appear that there was no significant difference between towns governed by municipal corporations and those governed by town commissioners, in terms of the standard of services provided. There were examples of good and bad government in both categories. As far as corporate towns were concerned, the commission of the inquiry into the local government of towns in 1877 found good management in Kilkenny, where every account except that for the public baths, which had never been a paying concern, showed a credit balance and where the sanitary work was 'very fairly attended to', and bad manangement in Clonmel where corporate property had been administered in the interest of members of the corporation and to the disadvantage of the public, and where 'much closer attention by the Corporation to sanitary works is required, as the sanitary condition is by no means satisfactory'.[57] Burke's history of Clonmel, written in 1907, noted that although the corporation owned a considerable estate around the town, the town derived little profit from it, the rental having 'long been misappropriated by corporate jobbery'. The rents reserved by the corporation represented less than one-quarter of the valuation.[58] The corporation had, however, undertaken some major works in the 1880s and 1890s, having spent £6,000 on the erection of a town hall in 1880, £18,437 on waterworks in 1892 and succeeding years, and £13,000 for the puchase of the gas works in 1894. These and other loans were consolidated in 1896 by floating a municipal stock for £49,000.[59]

One of the most important developments in municipal government in the period prior to the reorganisation of local government in 1898, was the granting of the municipal franchise to women in Belfast and in the townships of Kingstown and Blackrock. In Belfast women householders gained the vote in 1887 as the result of a local act introduced by the Belfast MPs, Sir James Corry, William Ewart and William Johnston.[60] This extended the franchise from male householders in properties rated at least £10 p.a., to every adult householder who had resided for one year within the borough itself or within seven miles of it. The act had been prompted by a plan formulated by Belfast Corporation to undertake a main drainage scheme in the city at a cost of around £300,000. Since such a scheme would affect every ratepayer, local MPs argued that the franchise should be extended to give ratepayers generally a voice in the control of expenditure. The original bill introduced for this purpose would have established household suffrage in all Irish boroughs, bringing Ireland into line with England in this respect, but in the face of fierce opposition within parliament the sponsors of the bill decided to limit it to Belfast.[61] Nationalist MPs who had long argued for household suffrage in Irish boroughs protested at the limitation but recognised that a wider measure would fail to get through parliament. If it passed the commons it would be certain to be thrown out by the lords.[62] The discussion of the measure in the lords reveals the criteria that were being used to judge Irish towns in terms of their fitness for household suffrage. Lord Erne announced that he

> held that it was most desirable, whenever possible, to assimilate the law in Ireland to that existing in England; and he thought that the ratepayers of a loyal, prosperous, and progressive community like Belfast were preeminently entitled to the same privileges as those enjoyed by their brethren on this side of the channel.[63]

During the progress of the bill through parliament a number of women active in the suffrage movement in the north took the opportunity to press the claims of Irish women to the municipal franchise, a privilege which their sisters in England had enjoyed since 1869 and those in Scotland since 1882. The North of Ireland Women's Suffrage Committee approached Corry and the other sponsors of the bill and persuaded them to substitute the word 'person' for 'man' in the clause defining qualified voters. To make absolutely sure that the bill would encompass women, an amendment was moved in the lords by Lord Erne adding an explanatory clause showing that the word 'person' was intended to include women. In a letter to the *Northern Whig* in July 1887 welcoming the admission of women to the 'most important of local franchises', Isabella M.S. Tod, who was both founder and secretary of the North of Ireland Women's Suffrage Committee, expressed the hope that in casting their votes women in Belfast would

> care less for mere party politics than men do, and more for the great social and moral questions which ought to be the end for which party politics are only the means. As they will now have a share in choosing the policy of the town and the men who are to carry it out, they can influence efficiently all matters concerning the peace and good order of the streets, the progress of sanitary reform, the cause of temperance, and other questions in which they have a vital interest.[64]

As a result of the Belfast act a considerable number of women became entitled to vote at muncipal elections in the city. 4,756 women were qualified to vote in Belfast in 1890,[65] and by 1895 this figure had risen to around 6,200, out of a total number of 38,000 municipal voters.[66] The number of women voters in Belfast was thus not far below the total number of voters in Dublin, where the municipal electorate comprised around 8,000 voters in contrast to the 37,000 entitled to vote at parliamentary elections.[67] Women became eligible to vote in the Dublin townships of Kingstown and Blackrock as the result of a local act passed in 1894. Those enfranchised by this measure were quick to exercise their new privilege. Of a total of 310 women qualified to vote in five wards contested in the following municipal election, around 220 did so.[68] The extension of the franchise in these cases was not specifically intended to benefit women, but their presence on registers of voters probably helped to ensure their general enfranchisement under the local government act of 1898.

Notes

1 Greer to Downshire, 27 Oct. 1811 (P.R.O.N.I., Downshire papers, D671/C/12/109).
2 Heads of the Newry police and navigation bill, 1824 (ibid, D671/C/12/292); Tony Canavan, *Frontier Town: An Illustrated History of Newry* (Belfast, 1989), p. 124.
3 Canavan, *Frontier Town*, p. 126; 9 Geo. IV c.82.
4 For a list of towns in Ireland with the acts under which they were governed, see *Report of the local government and taxation of towns inquiry commission, (Ireland)*, [C 1696], H.C. 1877, xxxix, iv. See also, *Special report by W.P. O'Brien to the lord lieutenant upon the local government and taxation of Ireland, made in pursuance of the report of the select committee of the house of commons dated 20th July1877*, [C 1965], H.C. 1878, xxiii, 792–796 (Appendix F: Return showing the names of each municipal town in Ireland, its area, population, and valuation; the act under which it is constituted; the number of members comprising its governing body; the number of counties, baronies and electoral divisions partly comprised in each, and the total expenditure for 1866 and 1876 respectively.)
5 Davison to Cramsie, 24 Feb. 1845 (P.R.O.N.I., Papers of Ballymoney town commissioners, D1518/4/1). Cramsie later became chairman of the Ballymoney commissioners.
6 D.G. Marnane, *Land and Violence: A History of West Tipperary from 1660* (Tipperary, 1985), p. 66. Marnane notes that in 1850, the first year for which records survive, the commissioners expended £50 on cleaning the town, £10 and £14 respectively on salaries for the clerk and the rate-collector and £6 on stationery. To cover these costs a rate was levied of 4d in the £ on houses with a yearly value of £5–£10, 6d on houses valued £10-£20 and 8d on houses valued at over £20.
7 17 & 18 Vict. c.103.
8 First annual report of the Ballymoney town commissioners, 3 May 1859 (P.R.O.N.I., Records of Ballymoney town commissioners, D1518/4/1).
9 First annual report of Lurgan town commissioners, 1856 (P.R.O.N.I., Lurgan town commissioners annual reports, T3077/1/1).
10 Ninth annual report of Lurgan town commissioners, 1864 (ibid., T3077/1/9).
11 *Report of the local government and taxation of towns inquiry commission, (Ireland)*, [C 1696], H.C. 1877, xxxix, 21.
12 Ibid., p. 21.
13 *Report from the select committee on local government and taxation of towns (Ireland)*, H.C. 1878 (262), xvi, 12.
14 *Report from the select committee on local government and taxation of towns (Ireland)*, H.C. 1877 (357), xl, 602.
15 *Report from the select committee on local government and taxation of towns (Ireland)*, H.C. 1878 (262) xvi, 15, 11.
16 43 Vict. c.17.
17 *Special report by W.P. O'Brien to the lord lieutenant upon the local government and taxation of Ireland, made in pursuance of the report of the select committee of the house of commons dated 20th July 1877*, [C 1965], H.C. 1878, xxiii, 757–758.
18 Ibid., 758.
19 *Report of the local government and taxation of towns inquiry commission, (Ireland)*, [C 1696], H.C. 1877, xxxix, 11–12.
20 Ibid., 22.
21 *Report from the select committee on local government and taxation of towns (Ireland)*, H.C. 1878 (262), xvi, 8; *Report of the local government and taxation of towns inquiry commission, (Ireland)*, [C 1696], H.C. 1877, xxxix, 17.

22 *Irish Times*, 11 Sept. 1865.
23 *Special report by W.P. O'Brien to the lord lieutenant upon the local government and taxation of Ireland*, [C 1965], H.C. 1878, xxiii, 747–749; W.F. Bailey, *Local and Centralized Government in Ireland*, p. 39.
24 *Annual report of the Local Government Board (Ireland)*, [C 967], H.C. 1874, xxvi, 32.
25 Petition of Ballymoney town commissioners, 15 Dec. 1887 (P.R.O.N.I., Records of Ballymoney town commissioners, D1518/4/1).
26 *Annual report of the Local Government Board (Ireland)*, [C 5769], H.C. 1889, xxxvi, 725.
27 See below, pp 95–97.
28 *Morning Post*, 19 June 1865.
29 *First report of the commissioners appointed to inquire into municipal corporations in Ireland*, H.C. 1835, xxvii, 23.
30 Ibid., 27.
31 Ibid., 523.
32 *Report from the commissioners appointed to inquire into municipal corporations (Ireland), Appendix, Part iii*, H.C. 1836, xxiv, 1176–1177.
33 Ibid., 633–641.
34 Cornelius O'Leary, 'Belfast Urban Government in the Age of Reform', in David Harkness and Mary O'Dowd (eds), *The Town in Ireland: Historical Studies xiii* (Belfast, 1981), pp 191–192.
35 *First report of the commissioners appointed to inquire into municipal corporations in Ireland; Appendix (report on Dublin)*, H.C. 1835, xxvii, 154–155.
36 Ibid., 159–160.
37 *Hansard 3*, xxix, 1312 (31 Jan. 1835).
38 Ibid., 1315, 1318.
39 Oliver MacDonagh, *The Emancipist: Daniel O'Connell 1830–1847* (New York, 1989), p. 152.
40 The franchise in Dublin was extended in 1849 to all male ratepayers who had been resident in the city for at least three years. The residency qualification was reduced to one year in 1876.
41 3 & 4 Vict. c.108.
42 39 & 40 Vict. c.76.
43 *Report from the select committee on local government and taxation of towns (Ireland)*, H.C. 1877 (357), xl, 469.
44 *Report of the local government and taxation of towns inquiry commission, (Ireland)*, [C 1696], H.C. 1877, xxxix, 5–6.
45 O'Leary, 'Belfast Urban Government in the Age of Reform', pp 196–197.
46 *Annual report of the local government board*, [C 967], H.C. 1874, xxvi, 32.
47 *Report from the select committee on local government and taxation of towns (Ireland)*, H.C. 1878 (262), xvi, 11. The corporation operated alongside the harbour commissioners and the water board. The latter was established in 1840 to take over responsibility for the water supply from the Belfast Charitable Society.
48 *Report from the select committee on local government and taxation of towns (Ireland)*, H.C. 1878 (262), xvi, 11.
49 Mary Daly, 'Late Nineteenth and Early Twentieth Century Dublin', in Harkness and O'Dowd (eds), *The Town in Ireland*, p. 245. Daly defends the corporation's record in public health matters, stressing the difficulties facing the authority given the abnormally high precentage of Dublin's population suffering from poor housing conditions and low wages and the slow rise in the city's valuation which restricted both rate levels and borrowing powers. The corporation initiated work on a project bringing water from the Vartry river in 1862, which gave Dublin the cheapest water scheme in the British Isles and although work on main drainage was

not begun until 1897, the corporation did address the problem of tenement housing, thought to be one of the main causes of the city's high rate of mortality, with some success. Ibid., pp 237–242.

50 MacDonagh, *The Emancipist*, pp 202–209.
51 Daly, 'Late Nineteenth and Early Twentieth century Dublin', pp 228–230.
52 *Daily Express*, 8 Mar. 1870.
53 *Report from the select committee on local government and taxation of towns (Ireland)*, H.C. 1877 (357), xl, 426.
54 Ibid., 426.
55 Ibid., 408–415.
56 Morrow to Hayes, 26 Nov. 1896 (S.P.O., Crime branch (special) files, S.12942).
57 *Report of the local government and taxation of towns inquiry commission, (Ireland)*, [C 1696], H.C. 1877, xxxix, 5–7.
58 W.P. Burke, *History of Clonmel* (Clonmel, 1907, reprinted Kilkenny, 1983), pp 233–235.
59 Ibid., p. 235.
60 50 & 51 Vict. c. cxviii.
61 *Hansard 3*, cccxiv, 1228–9 (6 May 1887).
62 Ibid., 1229–1230.
63 *Hansard 3*, cccxvi, 388 (17 June 1887).
64 *Northern Whig*, 23 July 1887.
65 Return to an order of the house of lords dated 25 July 1890 (Girton College, Cambridge, Helen Blackburn papers).
66 Edmund Harvey, 'The Position of Irishwomen in Local Administration', paper published by the Women's Emancipation Union, 1895, p. 2.
67 Daly, 'Late Nineteenth and Early Twentieth Century Dublin', p. 228.
68 Harvey, 'The Position of Irishwomen in Local Administration', p. 2.

SECTION III:

Local Government Act of 1898

An article on Irish local government in *The Spectator* in February 1888 complained that Parnellite talk of '[Dublin] Castle tyranny' had affected the way people thought about local government until 'we have really got to believe that local government is carried on in Ireland on some system far more centralised and far more despotic than in England', whereas in actual fact the two countries were governed on much the same system, and as far as county government was concerned, 'the Irish county system [of grand juries and presentment sessions] gives far more rights and far more power to the ratepayer than does the existing English arrangement, where none but the magistrates have anything to say as to how the county rate shall be expended'.[1] This was a valid argument but it was soon to lose its force. In October 1885 the conservative leader, Lord Salisbury, had pledged his party to reform county government throughout the United Kingdom and in March 1888 the conservative government introduced legislation creating elected county councils in England, Wales and Scotland. (An act creating district and parish councils followed in 1894.) Ministers accepted that with democratic local government established in England it was only a matter of time before Ireland would follow. Since both the liberal and conservative parties now supported the principle of local government reform in Ireland, the real questions were when it would happen and what form it would take. Pressure for reform was coming mainly from the liberal unionists, who had broken away from their own party after Gladstone's conversion to Home Rule and on whose support Salisbury's conservative government depended. But it was reform geared to Irish circumstances, not simply an extension of the English system, that the liberal unionists wanted, whereas English conservatives such as Salisbury and Arthur and Gerald Balfour, were primarily motivated by a desire to bring Irish legislation as closely into line with English as possible.[2] Nationalists regarded the issue of local government reform as a diversion and, whilst supporting reform in principle, were suspicious of proposals which were being advocated by some unionists as an alternative to Home Rule.

Although Ireland had been excluded from the local government reform of 1888 on the grounds that the agitation then disturbing the country made any such reform impossible, local government remained on the political agenda and in 1891 Arthur Balfour, then Irish chief secretary, announced that legislation would be introduced in the next session of parliament. The measure presented to the commons in February 1892 followed the English model in so far as it established county and district councils, elected on a parliamentary franchise, to which the administrative functions of grand juries together with some of the powers exercised by boards of guardians would be transferred, but it departed from the English measure in providing protection for minority (landlord and protestant) interests. The bill included cumulative voting, with extra votes for those paying the highest county cess, a power to dismiss any council on the petition of twenty cess payers in the event of illegal, corrupt or oppressive conduct, together with the creation of a joint committee of council members and grand jurors with a supervisory vote on both capital expenditure and appointments. Irish unionists supported the bill, but it aroused little enthusiasm elsewhere, being condemned by nationalist members as an insult to Ireland.[3] When local government reform resurfaced in 1897, it was as a device to break a parliamentary logjam. Irish members, unionist and nationalist, had united to demand recompense for the over-taxation of Ireland revealed by the royal commission on financial relations,[4] rejecting government proposals to use the money owing to establish a board of agriculture and to fund poor law reform. With the legislative programme under threat, the government announced that the board of agriculture and poor law bills would be dropped and a local government bill introduced, and promised a full grant equivalent to the over-taxation.[5]

Introducing the local government bill in the commons on 21 February 1898, the Irish chief secretary, Gerald Balfour, presented local government reform in Ireland as the inevitable consequence of reform in England and Scotland, referring to grand juries as 'no longer in harmony with the spirit of the age'. The grand jury system had, he said,

> no principle of growth in it. The tendency of the present day is to throw upon local bodies a number of duties which were never considered in connection with local administration a generation ago. You cannot put old wine into new bottles and in my judgement the reform of local administration in Ireland has now become almost a condition of the further reforms which I hope ultimately to see accomplished.[6]

The bill itself followed the English act as closely as possible, both as a matter of principle and convenience, but it did take account of the concerns of Irish landowners. Local government was to be distributed between county councils, urban and rural district councils and boards of guardians. Councillors were to be elected triennially, on a parliamentary franchise with the addition of women and peers. Plural voting was abolished, as were ex officio poor law guardians. The distinction between county cess and the poor rate was to cease. All previous local rates were to be consolidated into one rate collected by the county council. This rate was to fall entirely upon the occupier of land instead of partly upon the occupier and partly upon the owner as in the past. But in order to ease the burden the imperial exchequer was to distribute a sum equal to half the county cess and half the poor rate paid in the year 1896–97. In practice this meant that the government was taking over that portion of the rates previously paid by landlords (landowners had been responsible for half the poor rate of all their tenants together with the county cess on holdings worth less than £4 p.a.), and by so doing succeeded in reconciling large landowners to the reformed system. The interests of landowners were further protected by a number of restrictions on the new councils. Unlike county councils in England, they were not to be given control of the police, there was to be a statutory limit on the amount of road tax district councils might levy and clerics of all denominations were excluded from holding local government office. (Anyone who had served a prison sentence including hard labour within the previous five years was also excluded.) The bill met little opposition in parliament and passed into law on 12 August 1898.[7]

The structure of local administration which emerged from the reform of 1898 was not fundamentally different from that which had existed before. What had changed was the membership of local government bodies, particularly at county level. Whereas before 1898 county administration had been conducted by the grand jury and by magistrates and ratepayers at presentment sessions, with public health matters being taken care of by poor law guardians, the new system substituted county councils for grand juries while rural district councils took over from baronial presentment sessions and boards of guardians.[8] The county council was responsible for the upkeep of county institutions such as the courthouse, prison and infirmary together with main roads and important bridges, while the district council took care of more local matters such as minor roads and public works. Since the county council was the sole rating authority, expenditure by the rural district council had to be presented to and approved by the county council. Anyone elected to a rural district council served not only as a district councillor but also as a poor law guardian, so that separate elections for poor law guardians in rural areas disappeared. The rural district council automatically became the sanitary authority for the area. In order to provide a link between the district and the county, the chairman of the district council sat on the county council as an additional member. County councils were empowered to hold land for county purposes, to authorise outdoor relief to be administered by boards of guardians in the event of exceptional distress and to make by-laws. Dispensary committees were abolished and their functions transferred to the poor law boards. The grand jury retained its role in criminal matters, although applications for compensation for malicious injury were transferred to the county court with a right of appeal to a judge of assize.

The position of urban councils was largely unchanged by the act, except for the fact that they were elected under a wider franchise. In many cases town commissioners were already urban sanitary authorities. Under the act all towns and boroughs became urban districts, with the council as the roads and sanitary authority for the district. All business relating to the district, such as the upkeep of roads, previously transacted at presentment sessions or by the grand jury, with the exception of work chargeable on the county at large, was transferred to the urban district council together with the power to levy rates. Urban district councils were more independent of the county council than rural district councils, and the chairs were not empowered to sit as an additional member of the county council. Separate boards of guardians were retained in urban districts, elected on the same franchise as councillors.

From the point of view of women the act represented, in the words of Anna Haslam, 'the most significant political revolution that has taken place in the history of Irishwomen'.[9] Haslam had reason to sound a triumphant note since she had played a leading role in ensuring that women would be able to stand as well as vote in local elections. When the bill was first introduced, women had been excluded from membership of county councils and their position with regard to district councils was unclear. As a member of the committee of the Women's Local Government Society, Haslam worked with sympathetic MPs, such as William Johnston of Belfast, to amend the bill in order to clarify the position of women. By the time it reached the statute book, the bill (and the draft 'adaptation order' which accompanied it) included provisions entitling women who were qualified to vote under the act to stand for office as district councillors and as poor law guardians in urban districts. (In rural districts successful candidates served both as councillors and poor law guardians.) A residential qualification was secured for candidates for district councils, whereby persons who were not local government electors were eligible to stand as candidates if they had resided in the district for twelve months before the election and continued to reside. This provision was particularly important for enabling many married women to stand as district councillors, and Haslam proudly observed that 'we have it on the best authority that it was a letter from the [Women's

Local Government] Society which secured [for the amendment] the sympathy and support of the chief secretary for Ireland'.[10] The Society also lobbied vigorously, and successfully, for an amendment providing for two-membered constituencies for district councillors, without which, it was feared, women would be squeezed out of many elections since it was felt that 'the electors in a constituency would desire to elect a man to represent them in religion and politics, and only after that would they elect a woman to see to the sick poor'.[11] The work required for promoting the amendments, Haslam commented, had been considerable.

> About 300 copies of amendments were sent out to Irish Members and to other Members known to be sympathetic, and a great many letters were written to friendly societies and individuals, asking for support, special letters going to the women poor law guardians in Ireland.

Valuable support had been received from the Women's Liberal Unionist Association and the Scottish Women's Liberal Federation 'which sent out letters to every member of their own party representing a Scotch constituency'.[12] Although women were excluded from membership of county councils, Haslam was not too disappointed about this, arguing in her article in *The Englishwoman's Review* shortly after the passage of the act

> that there are certainly very few at present who would be willing to undertake that office; nor are its duties at all so well calculated to enlist their sympathies, or draw out their special gifts. And on the whole it is better that Ireland should not precede Great Britain in the extension of these franchises.[13]

The first elections under the act were held in March 1899. In December 1898, police officers were directed to include matters relating to the forthcoming elections in their monthly reports. A précis of such reports from January 1899 left little doubt that the elections would in most cases be a simple contest between nationalists/tenants and unionists/landlords. At a nationalist meeting in Maghera in County Londonderry, for example, the candidates selected to contest the division were required to sign a pledge

> that I will not on any occasion vote for a landlord, his nominee or an ex-grand juror being placed in any position of honor or trust in this district or county unless pledged to advocate the claims of Ireland to the right of a full measure of self-government. That in all matters affecting the well-being and to advance the interests of the nationalists generally, I will sit, act and vote with the majority of my colleagues in the district council.[14]

Addressing a nationalist meeting in Parsonstown in the King's County, the Rev. Dr Phelan advised those present to vote for nationalists only and not to give any support to unionists. Nationalist candi-

dates selected to represent the district and the county pledged themselves 'to support the interests of artisans and labourers, to vote for
every movement calculated to promote the cause of Home Rule, and
to support the catholic university movement'. The voice of modera-
tion was occasionally raised. In County Wexford, for example, a letter
appeared in the *New Ross Standard* on 17 December from the parish
priest of Ramsgrange, Canon Doyle, urging voters to exclude no man
on account of his creed and to elect none 'but steady, sensible men of
thoroughly practical habits'. But it is doubtful whether Canon Doyle's
strictures were any more effective than the attempts of a local magistrate to persuade nationalist ratepayers in the town of Monaghan to
select at least seven unionists out of a total of twenty-one candidates
for the town council. His proposal apparently gave rise to heated discussion and was rejected by a large majority. In some places, however,
voters put their pockets before politics. It was reported that at a meeting of ratepayers in the City of Waterford on 16 November, attended
by about a hundred men of all political shades, it was decided that candidates selected to represent the ratepayers' association should be
required to sign a pledge not to vote for any increase in salary of more
than £10 p.a. without the sanction of the association.[15]

The results of the elections caused little surprise. Nationalists took
around 75% of county council seats with 774 seats compared to 265
won by unionists, a major proportion of these being in Ulster. This
presented a stark contrast to the situation immediately prior to the
act, when unionists filled 704 grand jury places with only 47 occupied
by nationalists. [16] Four women were returned as urban district councillors and at least twenty-six as rural district councillors.[17] During the
debates on the act, government spokesmen had stressed that in their
view the success or failure of the new system would depend on the
degree to which the administrative experience of the local gentry was
utilised. If they were unable or unwilling to participate administrative
standards would suffer. In his speech introducing the bill, Gerald Balfour had expressed the hope that the Irish people would recognise the
gentry as their natural leaders as had happened in England and Scotland, to which an Irish member responded with a candid 'Not likely'.[18]
Balfour's wish to see the Irish gentry retain their leading role in local
government was to be disappointed but, in the early years of the system at least, the dire predictions of extravagance, jobbery and maladministration on the part of nationalist councils were not fulfilled. In
the period from 1899 to 1905, the reports of the Local Government
Board, which continued to supervise local administration, expressed
general satisfaction with the conduct of the new councils.[19] Officials at
Dublin Castle welcomed a reform which, in giving Ireland a coherent
and popularly acceptable system of local government, facilitated state

initiatives on matters such as poverty or economic development that required local co-operation.[20]

The changeover to the new system of local administration created by the local government act took place relatively smoothly, a tribute perhaps to the democratic spirit prevailing in Ireland. But it was also an indication of the degree to which local government had evolved since the beginning of the century. Much had changed. Urban administration had been reorganised and democratised and partly elected poor law boards made responsible for implementing a range of health and welfare legislation. Grand juries remained as a symbol of landlord domination of the countryside, but their powers were more closely regulated and less easily abused than had once been the case. And local government itself had changed. No longer a matter of landlords ensuring that estate roads were kept up, it involved the administration of increasingly complex legislation, supervised by an ever-growing army of officials. The local government act did deprive southern landlords of an important power base, but it was a base upon which their hold had been slipping for some time.

Notes

1 *The Spectator*, 18 Feb. 1888.
2 C.B. Shannon, The Ulster liberal unionists and local government reform, 1885–98', *Irish Historical Studies*, xviii (March 1973), 407–423; Andrew Gailey, *Ireland and the Death of Kindness: the experience of constructive unionism 1890–1905* (Cork, 1987), pp 441–42.
3 Shannon, 'The Ulster liberal unionists and local government reform', 415–418; Alvin Jackson, *The Ulster Party: Irish Unionists in the House of Commons, 1884–1911* (Oxford, 1989), pp 170–172.
4 *Report of the royal commission appointed to inquire into the financial relations of Great Britain and Ireland*, [C 8262], H.C. 1896, xxxiii.
5 Gailey, *Ireland and the Death of Kindness*, pp 45–46.
6 *Hansard 4*, liii, 1227 (21 Feb. 1898).
7 61 & 61 Vict. c.37.
8 See Appendix VII. See also J. Muldoon and G. M'Sweeny, *A Guide to Irish Local Government* (Dublin, 1899).
9 Anna Haslam, 'Irishwomen and Local Government Act', *The Englishwoman's Review*, 15 Oct. 1898.
10 Women's Local Government Society, Sixth annual report, 1899, p. 8.
11 Ibid., p. 8.
12 Ibid., p. 8.
13 Haslam, 'Irishwomen and the Local Government Act', *The Englishwoman's Review*, 15 Oct. 1898.
14 Precis of files relative to the forthcoming elections under the local government act of 1898, Jan. 1899 (S.P.O., Crime branch (special) files, S/18000).
15 Ibid.
16 Pauric Travers, *Settlements and Divisions: Ireland 1870–1922* (Dublin, 1988), p. 66.
17 Women's Association of Poor Law Guardians, seventeenth annual report, 1899, p. 9.
18 *Hansard 4*, liii, 1248 (21 Feb. 1898).
19 Catherine Shannon, 'Local Government in Ireland, the Politics and Administration', M.A. thesis (U.C.D., 1963), pp 310–11.
20 Gailey, *Ireland and the Death of Kindness*, p. 49.

Appendix I:
Lords Lieutenant of Counties 1831–1850

County	First appointee	Subsequent appointees
Antrim	Earl O'Neil	Earl of Belfast
		(Marq. of Donegal)
Armagh	Earl of Gosford	Col. J. Caulfield
Carlow	Visct. Duncannon	Hon. J. Ponsonby
Cavan	Marq. of Headfort	
Clare	Lord Fitzgerald and	
	Vesci	Sir Lucius O'Brien
Cork	Earl of Shannon	Earl of Bandon
Donegal	Marq. of Donegal	Marq. of Abercorn
Down	Marq. of Downshire	Lord Castlereagh
Dublin	Earl of Meath	
Fermanagh	Earl of Enniskillen	Earl of Erne
Galway	Marq. of Clanricarde	
Kerry	Earl of Kenmare	
Kildare	Duke of Leinster	
Kilkenny	Marq. of Ormonde	1. Visct. Duncannon
		2. Rt Hon W. Tighe
King's Co.	Lord Oxmantown	
	(Earl of Rosse)	
Leitrim	Earl of Leitrim	
Limerick	Hon R. Fitzgibbon	Earl of Clare
Londonderry	Lord Garvagh	Sir R. Ferguson
Longford	Lord Forbes	1. Luke White
		2. Col. H. White
Louth	Sir Patrick Bellew	
	(Lord Bellew)	
Mayo	Marq. of Sligo	Earl of Lucan
Meath	Earl Darnley	1. Lord Dunsany
		2. Earl of Fingall
Monaghan	Lord Rossmore	Hon R Westenra
		(Lord Rossmore)
Queen's Co.	Visct. de Vesci	
Roscommon	Visct. Lorton	
Sligo	Col. Arthur Knox Gore	
Tipperary	Earl of Donoghmore	
Tyrone	Earl of Caledon	Earl of Charlemont
Waterford	Henry Villiers Stuart	
	(Lord Stuart de Decies)	
Westmeath	Marq. of Westmeath	
Wexford	R.S. Carew (Lord Carew)	
Wicklow	Earl of Wicklow	

County of City/Town

Carrickfergus	Earl O'Neil	Earl of Belfast
		(Marq. of Donegal)
Cork	Earl of Shannon	Earl of Bandon
Galway	Marq. of Clanricarde	
Dublin	Earl of Meath	
Drogheda	Sir Patrick Bellew	
	(Lord Bellew)	
Waterford	Henry Villiers Stuart	
	(Lord Stuart of Decies)	
Londonderry	Lord Garvagh	Sir R. Ferguson

Source: Clarendon Papers (Irish), Box 33

Appendix II:
Local Government Offices in Limerick in 1892

Her Majesty's Lieutenant of the County and Costos Rotulorum
High Sheriff
Deputy-Lieutenants
County Court Judge and Chairman of Quarter Sessions
Magistrates
Resident Magistrates

County Officers:

Clerk of the Crown and Peace
Registrar of Civil Bill Court
Crown Solicitor
Sessional Crown Solicitor
Sessional Crown Prosecutor
Treasurer
Secretary to the Grand Jury
Clerk to Secretary
County Surveyors
Assistant Surveyors
Sub-Sheriff
Sheriff's Returning Officer
Notaries Public
Coroners
Barony Cess Collectors

Stamp Distributors

H.M. District Male Prison:

Visiting Committee
Governor
Chief Warder
Church of Ireland Chaplain
R.C. Chaplain
Physician
Apothecary

County Infirmary:

Treasurer
Surgeon
Physician
Resident Apothecary
Secretary
Matron

County Lunatic Asylum:
Board of Governors
Medical Superintendent
Visiting Physician
Church of Ireland Chaplain
R.C. Chaplain
Apothecary
Matron
Clerk
Storekeeper

Inspectors of National Schools

Poor Law Unions:
Treasurer
Clerk and Returning Officer
Master and Matron
Chaplains
Medical Officer
Relieving Officers
Superintendent Registrar of Births, Deaths and Marriages
Dispensary District Medical Officers
Consulting Sanitary Officer
Executive Sanitary Officer
Sanitary Officers
Sanitary Sub-Officers

Source: *Thom's Official Directory . . . for the year 1892* (Dublin, 1892).

Appendix III:
Grand Jury of County Antrim, Lent Assizes 1847

Nathaniel Alexander, Foreman
Sir Edmund Macnaghten
George Macartney
John Cromie
John Rowan
Conway Dobbs
John M'Neile
John Montgomery
James S. Moore
James Agnew
John White
Hugh Lecky
William Agnew
George Moore
George J. Clarke
Hon. George Handcock
Thomas Verner
Charles W. Armstrong
John J. Burnett
John Harrison
Peter M'Garel
Thomas R Stannus
H.H.H. O'Hara

Source: P.R.O.N.I., Grand Jury Records, ANT 4/7/3

Appendix IV:
Board of Guardians for the Carrick-on-Suir Poor Law Union, County Tipperary, 1889

Elected Guardians:

John Gready
William White
Michael Hickey
Thomas Rockett
Peter Wall
Michael Wall
James Fitzgerald
A. English
Thomas McGrath
Michael Power
John Wallace
Thomas Power
John Thompson
William Wall
Walter Walsh
Daniel Butler
William Malcomson
Jeramiah Nugent
Maurice Burke
Thomas Bowers
John Keeffe
Robert Barry

Ex-officio Guardians:

Earl Of Bessborough
A.E. Caldecott
Thomas Lalor
S.J. Lynch
O. Mansfield
J.T. Medlycott
C. Morley
Michael Morris
Redmond O'Donnell
J.H. Power
E. Quinn
H.J.R.V. Stuart
F. Weldon Walshe
Marquis of Waterford
G.W. Withers
John Barnes
C.P. Bolton
W.N. Barron
Viscount Clifden
Earl of Clonmell
A. Congreve
Marquis of Ormonde
N.A. Power
Sir R.C. Power

Chairman: Thomas McGrath
Vice-Chairman: Michael Power
Deputy Vice-Chairman: John Wallace

Board meets every Saturday

Source: *County Tipperary One Hundred Years Ago, a guide and directory, 1889,* by George Henry Bassett (reprinted Belfast, 1991), pp 203–204.

Appendix V:
Town Commissioners of Westport, County Mayo, 1892

William Livingstone, Chairman
Lord J.T. Browne, D.L.
The Marquess of Sligo
Arthur O'Malley
William Horkan
Thomas Murray
John Mulloy
John Walsh
Henry Horan

Patrick Toole
Patrick Heraty
Austin O'Malley
Thomas Joyce
Martin J. M'Hale
Peter J. Kelly
Owen O'Malley
James Moran
William Scott

Town Clerk: Francis Egan

Source: *Thom's Official Directory . . . for the year 1892* (Dublin, 1892), p. 1254.

Appendix VI:
Dublin Municipal Corporation, 1850

Lord Mayor – John Reynolds M.P.

Aldermen:

Henry Bowles
Luke Butler
James Fallon
Charles Gavin
Edward Hudson
John Keshan
R.H. Kinahan
Robert M'Kenna

Cornelius M'Loghlin
James Moran
T. O'Brien M.P.
James Rooney
William Reynolds
Michael Staunton
Philip Tagart

Councillors

John Martin
Arthur Barlow
Henry Gore Carolan
Gustavus Hamilton
J. Reynolds
Lynn Carew
George White
Samuel Wauchoo
John Lee Wharton
Ambrose Sullivan
Peter Byrne
James Lambert
John Fortune
Martin Burke
James M'Carthy
Cornelius Denehy
George Gilcreest
Jeremiah Dunne
Maurice O'Connell
John Ryan
Edward Galavan
John Ferguson
John Radley
Richard Keating

Thomas Leech
James Fitzsimon
John O'Neill
Francis Tuite
John Healy
James Plunkett
Edward Reilly
Patrick Dunne
James Bury
Bartholomew Andrews
James Sheridan
Patrick Dowling
John M'Kenna
H. Curran
Myles Tobyn
Enoch Mack
Richard A. Walker
F.E. Thomas
M.P. James Delaney
T. Kirwan
R. Kelly

Source: *The Dublin Pictorial Guide & Directory of 1850, Henry Shaw* (reprinted Belfast, 1988).

Appendix VII:
Local Government before and after 1898

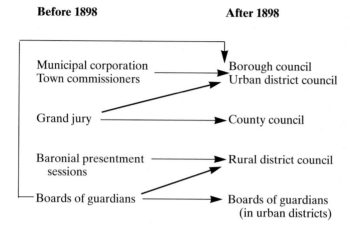

Before 1898   **After 1898**

Municipal corporation   Borough council
Town commissioners ————▶ Urban district council

Grand jury ————————————▶ County council

Baronial presentment ——————▶ Rural district council
   sessions

Boards of guardians ———————▶ Boards of guardians
                           (in urban districts)

Bibliography

A. Manuscript Sources

Abercorn papers, P.R.O.N.I.
Anglesey papers, P.R.O.N.I.
Ballymoney town commissioners papers, 1830–1893, P.R.O.N.I.
Belmore papers (appointed deputy lieutenant of County Tyrone 1856 and
    lord lieutenant of County Tyrone 1892), P.R.O.N.I.
Blackburn papers, Girton College, Cambridge
Boards of guardians records, P.R.O.N.I.
Browne papers (papers of 2nd Marquess of Sligo), N.L.I.
Brownlow papers, P.R.O.N.I.
Caledon papers (letter book of Lord Caledon as governor of County Tyrone
    1806–31 and as lord lieutenant of County Tyrone 1831–39), P.R.O.N.I.
Carew papers, T.C.D.
Carlisle papers (papers of 7th Earl of Carlisle, chief secretary, as Lord
Morpeth, 1835–41), Castle Howard, Yorkshire
Clarendon papers, Bodleian Library, Oxford
William Sharman Crawford papers, P.R.O.N.I.
Crime branch (special) files, S.P.O.
Derby papers, (papers of 14th Earl of Derby, chief secretary 1830–33 as
    Edward Stanley), Liverpool Record Office
Downshire papers, P.R.O.N.I.
Dufferin papers (lord lieutenant of County Down in 1860s), P.R.O.N.I.
Erne papers, P.R.O.N.I.
Fitzgerald papers, N.L.I.
Foster/Masserene papers, P.R.O.N.I
Grand jury records, P.R.O.N.I.
Hatherton papers (papers of 1st Baron Hatherton, chief secretary 1833–34 as
    Edward Littleton), Staffordshire County Record Office
Home Office papers, P.R.O.
Larcom papers, N.L.I.
Lurgan town commissioners annual reports, 1854-1868, P.R.O.N.I.
Monteagle papers, N.L.I.
Montgomery papers, P.R.O.N.I.
Newport papers, Queens University Belfast
Peel papers, B.L.
Registered papers, S.P.O.
Russell papers, P.R.O.
County Sligo grand jury resolution book, 1836–1871, N.L.I.
Vestry book of Arboe, County Tyrone, 1773–1833, P.R.O.N.I.
Vestry minute book of Greyabbey, County Down, 1789–1823, P.R.O.N.I.
Vestry minute book of Derrykeighan, County Antrim, 1802–1826, P.R.O.N.I.
Wellesley papers, B.L.

B. Parliamentary Debates and Papers

Hansard's parliamentary debates, 1st, 2nd, 3rd and 4th series, 1803–1908.

Report from the select committee on grand jury presentments of Ireland, H.C. 1814–15 (283), vi.

Report of the select committee on Irish grand jury presentments, H.C. 1816 (374), ix, *Second report*, H.C. 1816 (435), ix.

Report form the committee on grand jury presentments in Ireland, H.C. 1819 (378), viii.

First report from the select committee on grand jury presentments, Ireland, H.C. 1822 (353), vii.

Fifteenth report of the commissioners appointed to inquire into the duties, salaries and emoluments of the officers, clerks and ministers of justice in all temporal and ecclesiastical courts in Ireland: the office of sheriff, H.C. 1826 (310) xvii.

Report from the select committee on grand jury presentments, Ireland, H.C. 1826–7 (555), iii.

Names of all stipendiary magistrates in Ireland with the dates of their appointment and the counties in which they have served . . . , H.C. 1831–2 (360), xxxiii.

Correspondence relative to the late elections in Ireland, H.C. 1835 (170), xlv.

First report of the commissioners appointed to inquire into the municipal corporations in Ireland, H.C. 1835 (23), xxvii, *Supplement to the first report*, H.C. 1835 (24, 27, 28), xxvii; 1836 (29), xxiv.

Report of the select committee appointed to inquire into the duties, salaries and fees of officers paid by counties in Ireland, and into the presentments compulsory upon grand juries there and to report their opinion thereon . . . , H.C. 1836 (527), xii.

Report by the lords' select committee appointed to inquire into the state of Ireland since the year 1835, in respect of crime and outrage, H.C. 1839 (486), xii.

Report of the commissioners appointed to revise the several laws under or by virtue of which monies are now raised by grand jury presentments in Ireland, H.C. 1842 (386), xxiv.

A return of dates on which and the places where military and police have been employed in enforcing the collection of poor rates in Ireland, between the 1st January 1843 and the 1st January 1844, H.C. 1844 (186), xl, p. 785.

Report from the select committee on parliamentary and municipal elections, H.C. 1868–9 (352), viii.

Annual report of the Local Government Board (Ireland), [C 967], H.C. 1874, xxvi.

Report of the local government and taxation of towns inquiry commission, (Ireland), [C 1696], H.C. 1877, xxxix.

Report from the select committee on local government and taxation of towns (Ireland), H.C. 1877 (357), xl.

Report from the select committee on local government and taxation of towns (Ireland), H.C. 1878 (262), xvi.

Special report by W.P. O'Brien to the lord lieutenant upon the local government and taxation of Ireland, made in pursuance of the report of the select committee of the house of commons dated 20th July 1877, [C 1965], H.C. 1878, xxiii.

Annual report of the Local Government Board (Ireland), [C 5769], H.C. 1889, xxxvi.

Report of the royal commission appointed to inquire into the financial relations of Great Britain and Ireland, [C 8262], H.C. 1896, xxxiii.

Report of the royal commission on the poor laws and relief of distress: report on Ireland, [C 4630], H.C. 1909, xxxviii.

C. Newspapers
Belfast Newsletter
Connaught Journal
Dublin Evening Mail
Dublin Evening Post
Enniskillen Chronicle
Freeman's Journal
Irish Times
Kilkenny Journal
Limerick Chronicle
Limerick Times
Morning Post
Northern Whig
Sligo Independent
The Spectator
Strabane Morning Post
Tralee Chronicle

D. Dissertations
Grey, Peter, 'British Politics and the Ireland Question, 1843–1850', Ph.D. thesis (Cambridge University, 1992).

Flynn, P., 'A Study of Local Government in Galway in the Early Nineteenth Century', M.A. thesis (U.C.G., 1981).

Nolan, D., 'The Cork Grand Jury 1836–1899', M.A. thesis (U.C.G., 1974).

Rafferty, J., 'Local Administration in the Irish Counties prior to 1800 with particular reference to the period 1600–1800', M. Com. Sc. thesis (Q.U.B., 1932).

Shannon, Catherine, 'Local Government in Ireland, the Politics and Administration', M.A. thesis (U.C.D., 1963).

E. Nineteenth-Century Printed Works
William Carleton, *Valentine M'Clutchy: the Irish Agent; or, chronicles of the Castle Cumber property* (Dublin, 1845).

[Doyle, J.W., Bishop of Kildare and Leighlin], *Letters on the State of Ireland, by J.K.L.* (Dublin, 1825).

Edgeworth, Maria, *The Absentee* (1812, paperback edn. Oxford, 1988).

'Grand Jury Laws and Public Works', *Dublin University Magazine*, xxvii (1846), 346–355.

Hall, T.D., *Report on the state and progress of public buildings . . . in the county of Leitrim, as submitted to the Grand Jury at the spring assizes, 1838* (Dublin, 1838).

Harvey, Edmund, 'The Position of Irishwomen in Local Administration', paper published by the Women's Emancipation Union, 1895.

Haslam, Anna, 'Irishwomen and the Local Government Act', *The English-woman's Review*, 15 Oct. 1898.

'Irish Grand Juries: Mr Stanley's Bill', *The Metropolitan*, iv, (June 1832), 137–146.

'Irish Municipal Government', *Westminister Review*, xlviii (1847), 82–109.

Lindsay, H.L., *The present state of the Irish grand jury law considered as it respects the promotion and execution of public works and an improved plan of jurisprudence recommended* (Armagh, 1837).

Muldoon, J. and M'Sweeny, G., *A Guide to Irish Local Government* (Dublin, 1899).

Murphy, W., *Remarks on the Irish Grand Jury System . . .* (Cork, 1849).

Staples, Robert, 'Local Government in Ireland', *The Fortnightly Review*, xlvi (1886), 105–113.

The Parliamentary Gazetteer of Ireland (Edinburgh, 1844)

Thomas Rice, *An Inquiry into the Effect of the Irish Grand Jury Laws, as affecting the Industry, the Improvement, and the Moral Character of the People of England'* (2nd ed., London, 1815).

Edward Wakefield, *An Account of Ireland, Statistical and Political* (London, 1812).

F. Twentieth-Century Printed Works

Burke, Helen, *The People and the Poor Law in 19th Century Ireland* (Little-hampton, 1987).

Burke, W.P., *History of Clonmel* (Clonmel, 1907, reprinted Kilkenny, 1983).

Canavan, Tony, *Frontier Town: An Illustrated History of Newry* (Belfast, 1989).

Clark, Samuel, *Social Origins of the Irish Land War* (Princeton, 1979).

Crookshank, Anne, 'The Visual Arts, 1740–1850', in T.W. Moody and W.E. Vaughan (eds), *Eighteenth-Century Ireland 1691–1800* (Oxford, 1986), pp 471–541.

Daly, Mary, E., 'Late Nineteenth and Early Twentieth Century Dublin', in Harkness and O'Dowd (eds), *The Town in Ireland* (Belfast 1981), pp 221–252.

Daly, Mary E., *Dublin – The Deposed Capital: A Social and Economic History 1860–1914* (Cork, 1985).

Daly, Mary E., *The Famine in Ireland* (Dublin, 1986).

Deegan, Thomas, 'Roscrea Poor Law Union: its administration 150 years ago', *Tipperary Historical Journal 1992*, 96–104.

Edwards, R.D. and Williams, T.D. (eds), *The Great Famine: Studies in Irish History 1845–52* (Dublin, 1956).

Falkiner, C.L., *The Counties of Ireland: an historical sketch of their origin, constitution and gradual delimitation* (Dublin, 1903).

Feingold, William, 'The Tenants' Movement to Capture the Irish Poor Law Boards, 1877–1886', *Albion*, vii (1976), 216–231.

Feingold, W.L., *The Revolt of the Tenantry: the transformation of local government in Ireland 1872–86* (Boston, 1984).

Gailey, Andrew, *Ireland and the Death of Kindness: the experience of constructive unionism 1890-1905* (Cork, 1987).

Harkness, David and O'Dowd, Mary (eds), *The Town in Ireland: Historical Studies xiii* (Belfast, 1981).

Hawkins, R.A.J., 'An Army on Police Work, 1881-2: Ross of Blandensburg's memorandum, dated 11 Dec. 1882', *Irish Sword*, xi (1973), 75-117.

Hoppen, K.T., *Elections, Politics and Society in Ireland 1832–1885* (Oxford, 1984).

Jackson, Alvin, *The Ulster Party: Irish Unionists in the House of Commons, 1884-1911* (Oxford, 1989).

Kinealy, Christine, 'The Poor Law during the Great Famine: An Administration in Crisis', in E.M. Crawford, *Famine: the Irish Experience 900–1900* (Edinburgh, 1989), pp 157–175.

MacDonagh, Oliver, *The Emancipist: Daniel O'Connell 1830–1847* (New York, 1989).

McDowell, R.B., 'Ireland on the eve of the Famine', in R.D. Edwards and T.D. Williams, *The Great Famine* (Dublin, 1956), pp 3–86.

McDowell, R.B., *The Irish Administration 1801–1914* (London, 1964).

Marnane, D.G., *Land and Violence: A History of West Tipperary from 1660* (Tipperary, 1985).

Meghen, P.J., 'The Administrative Work of the Grand Jury', *Administration*, 6, (1958-59), 247-264.

Nelson, Thomas, *The Land War in County Kildare* (Maynooth, 1985).

O'Brien, Gerard, 'The establishment of poor-law unions in Ireland, 1838–43', *Irish Historical Studies*, xxiii, no. 90 (November 1982), 97–120.

O'Cinneide, S., *A Law for the Poor* (Dublin, 1970).

O'Connell, M.R., (ed.), *The Correspondence of Daniel O'Connell* (Dublin, 1972-80).

O'Donnell, Sean, 'The first election to the reformed Clonmel Corporation 150 years ago', *Tipperary Historical Journal 1992*, 75–80.

O Grada, Cormac, *The Great Irish Famine* (London, 1989).

O'Leary, Cornelius, 'Belfast Urban Government in the Age of Reform', in David Harkness and Mary O'Dowd (eds), *The Town in Ireland: Historical Studies xiii* (Belfast, 1981), pp 187–202.

O'Neill, T.P., 'The Organization and administration of Relief, 1845–52', in R.D. Edwards and T.D. Williams, *The Great Famine* (Dublin, 1956), pp 209–259.

O'Sullivan, H., 'The Court House, Dundalk and the Contract for its Erection Dated 30th April, 1813, *County Louth Archeological Journal*, xv, (1962), 131–143.

Roche, Desmond, *Local Government in Ireland* (Dublin, 1982).

Shannon, C.B., The Ulster liberal unionists and local government reform, 1885-98', *Irish Historical Studies*, xviii (March 1973), 407–423.

Travers, Pauric, *Settlements and Divisions: Ireland 1870-1922* (Dublin, 1988).

Walker, B.M. (ed.), *Parliamentary Election Results in Ireland, 1801–1922* (Dublin, 1978).

Webb, J.J., *Municipal Government in Ireland – Medieval and Modern* (Dublin, 1918).